LIFE AND TEACHING OF THE MASTERS OF THE FAR EAST

By Baird T. Spalding

Volume IV

 DeVorss *Publications*

Volume 4
ISBN: 0-87516-366-1

5 Volume Set
ISBN: 0-87516-538-9

DeVorss & Company, Publisher
P.O. Box 550
Marina del Rey, CA 90294

Printed in the United States of America

THE LIFE AND TEACHING
OF THE
MASTERS OF THE FAR EAST

by Baird T. Spalding

Baird T. Spalding, whose name became legend in metaphysical and truth circles during the first half of the 20th century, played an important part in introducing to the Western world the knowledge that there are Masters, or Elder Brothers, who are assisting and guiding the destiny of mankind. The countless numbers of letters that have come in through the years, from all over the world, bear testimony of the tremendous help received from the message in these books.

Partial listing of the contents of the five volumes:

Volume I: Introduction of the Master Emil—Visit to the "Temple of Silence"—Astral projection—Walking on Water—Visit to the Healing Temple—Emil talks about America—The Snowmen of the Himalayas—New Light on the teachings of Jesus.

Volume II: Visit to the Temple of the Great Tau Cross—Visit with the Master Jesus—Jesus discusses the nature of hell; the nature of God—The Mystery of thought vibrations—Jesus feeds the multitude—An account of a healing experience—Jesus and Buddha visit the group.

Volume III: One of the masters speaks of the Christ consciousness—The nature of cosmic energy—The creation of the planets and the worlds—The trip to Lhasa—Visit at the Temple Pora-tat-sanga—Explaining the mystery of levitation—A doubter becomes convinced of the existence of Jesus.

Volume IV: This material was first presented as "The India Tour Lessons." Each chapter has text for study, as well as guides to teachers for developing and interpreting the material. Among subjects covered: The White Brotherhood—The One Mind—Basis of coming social reorganization—Prana.

Volume V: Material taken from lectures given by Mr. Spalding in California during the last two years of his life. There is also a brief biographical sketch. Partial contents: Camera of past events—Is there a God—The divine pattern—The reality—Mastery over death—The law of supply.

Each of the 5 volumes has approximately 175 pages.

PUBLISHER'S NOTE

Both Mr. Spalding and Mr. DeVorss (who knew Mr. Spalding personally) died in the 1950's. The people who were associated with Mr. Spalding on the tour have also passed on. We are therefore without contact with anyone who has firsthand knowledge of the work, and the books themselves are now the only source of information. To our knowledge, there is no map available of the tour, and we know of no photographs. We have tried at various times to locate additional records, as well as camera information, but without success. We sincerely regret that we have no additional information to offer.

DEVORSS & COMPANY

CHAPTER I

GREAT WHITE BROTHERHOOD AND WORLD PEACE

1. Before going further in the study of certain underlying laws and facts regarding the teachings of the Masters, it is well to consider the scope their vision covers. One must enlarge his mind and outlook upon life to that in which the Masters work in order to fully understand the full purport of their teachings. At this time we will deal chiefly with the field to be taken into consideration and the general trends of mankind in order that we may fully adapt ourselves to the work that is before us. It is necessary to know the nature and scope of a field of work before selecting the tools and laying down a plan for tending the field. We must know to what the field is adapted, what crops are to be raised, and to what end the cultivation is to be directed. There must be a purpose back of all work and it is far beyond the reaches of what we commonly call our own individual nature. Each man's nature in one way and another is vitally associated with the life and well-being of every other individual in the world and what affects one must in some degree affect the rest of humanity.

2. I rather feel that this discussion of peace should be very general because everyone is interested. The fact is that the world is becoming peace-minded and that people are saying that we have had enough of war. People are beginning to understand that war is not a natural condition and to understand that all those who assume the role of

providence by setting themselves up as the embodiment of perfect Justice—the creators of Happiness —are only deceivers. Peace and Happiness, the heart's desire of all Humanity is not a gift to be bestowed upon mankind, but has to be earned by honest effort. There is not such a thing as political miracles. Man has to realize that he alone has the power to work out his destiny with his own intelligence.

3. This sweeping tide of human interest in that which will promote and guarantee peace is the inevitable working out of the Universal Law which always moves to promote the common good. God is no respecter of persons and this awakening of men along peace lines is their response to the movement of the Spirit of Peace which is fostered by the Masters. Only as the individual identifies himself with Universal Law can he expect to find his individual good for it is inseparably united with the common good. For this reason, true progress is slow and suffering is great.

4. There is a great brotherhood throughout the world who have been working for peace for thousands of years. They are back of every movement for world peace and are becoming stronger and stronger all the time. There are now about 216 groups throughout the world. There is always one central unit as a first or centralizing body and twelve units which surround that unit, giving it more force and power. They are working also for the enlightenment of the whole world.

5. These groups are really composed of human beings who are actuated by the high thought of the White Brotherhood. All of these groups work together. There is a very strong thought coming to the whole world for peace and enlightenment as well.

6. There are many misconceptions regarding the White Brotherhood. It must first be understood that they never make themselves known as such, nor are they exclusively back of any outer organization or organizations. They are Universal in their function and purpose. They definitely work with the Universal Law to universal ends and any individual or group working toward the same ends without selfish or group motives may receive their full support. This support may be known on the part of the man but it is more likely to come in the form of an unknown stimulus. That is, the help is not likely to assume the form of that coming from any definite place or person. Those receiving this support are conscious only of the help or influence.

7. The League of Nations originally was an instrument of the White Brotherhood but it was misused in many ways by certain nations and individuals. It will, however, come back under the guidance of the Brotherhood some time in the future.

8. The birth of a new order is in process; we are witnessing right now the destruction of an old civilization. The White Brotherhood will assert itself positively on the most important issues when the time is propitious.

9. The time has come when there can be no halfway ground in this purification of the race, whether or not individuals or groups array themselves against the common good in this day. The mills of God grind swiftly at times and also finely. Only from the siftings shall the selfish and aggressively grasping rear a new life's structure. It were far better to unify oneself with purely creative motives that contribute to universal good, for thereby shall good come to the individual.

10. Often the influences working in Universal

ideas come into being without much notice. It is something that seems to germinate and move forward as a contagion while the minds of many are still so engrossed in other things that they do not notice the change. Then, all of a sudden, each individual seems to realize that it has come into being and that it is in exact accord with his own secret thoughts. Thus, he very often slips into the new order rather unknowingly. The point is to be alert to these secretly developing forces within oneself and in the race, and here one will find the key to his most rapid progress and most vital service in the universal cause.

11. India has maintained peace by using methods identical to those used by these 216 groups about which I have spoken. It was brought about originally by twelve groups which have expanded and are still expanding. The influence of these bodies has been very great, entering into the whole fabric of Indian thought. Their work from the outer point of view has been largely educational. They release information orally which is acted upon under their direction. Results prove the efficacy of this method.

12. Gandhi studied the situation of non-violence for twenty years before he began his work, becoming a very deep student of it. The principle has been in existence in India for 600 years. Because of the Untouchables it was made operative through Gandhi in this generation. Gandhi went among the Untouchables, teaching non-violence, making it an effective force. The younger generation took it up immediately. They recognized the great effect of it and it spread throughout all India. The younger generation now have brought it before the people stronger than ever. This will eventually result in the dissolution of the caste system. The Untouchables became quite an issue there as they numbered some 65,000,-000 and guidance was necessary because they had

such powerful influence. Gandhi has been almost entirely responsible for their present emancipation.

13. Those in the groups mentioned that are working for world peace are persons of a very high spiritual understanding. One man of each group is always prominent as one of spiritual attainment.

14. There are some sixty in the United States who definitely belong to this association. They are very quiet concerning their connection with it. They do not give out the place of their group meetings or any information concerning their activities.

15. This is why many people are more or less incredulous concerning the great work being done by the illumined. They are so accustomed to outer show and display that they cannot imagine any great work being done in such a quiet, simple manner. But if one will stop to think for just a moment he will realize that all the motivating forces of the Universe are silent and those who work consciously with these forces move according to motives. There will come a time, however, when they will work more openly, but that will be when there are enough illumined people to know and understand just what they are doing. Study your own experiences. Are you not aware that silent influences working underneath the surface of your own being are those forces which control your life more than the outwardly manifest things which you express in words? However, just as these silent "broodings" of your own inner nature eventually find their outer expression when you are in an environment which harmonizes with them, you do not hesitate to express them. Study yourself and you will find everything working in you just as it is in the race. "What the Father sees in secret, He will reward you openly" is not an idle statement but it reveals the manner in which all things come into being in the outer world. To understand this fact will

not only be to better understand yourself but also the manner of the universal spiritual work that is going on underneath the surface all the time. It is only through adapting oneself to this sort of conscious procedure that he will be able to clearly trace the workings of the Secret Brotherhood. Their activities are hidden only to those who do not discern the mode of accomplishment. We are accustomed to noise and display and the quiet yet most powerful forces in ourselves and the world about us go unnoticed. We follow the noisy people into bypaths and lose the path of life that moves in stillness through our own individual being.

16. This Brotherhood is not properly an organization, as anyone can belong who will work constructively either openly or silently for peace. It is rather an association of kindred spirits. They co-operate, in fact, with any association or organization that is for the benefit of mankind or the advancement of humanity.

17. The group in India works silently but it is its influence that brings these bodies together and co-ordinates their activities. It was the activity of this very group that brought the Nobel Peace Prize before the world.

18. Tolstoy was a great factor in making this principle practically effective. But it has always been presented through the nine rulers of India. Tolstoy was an advanced soul. He was working with the great Central Group all the time.

19. While no one knows its exact location, that Thirteenth Group has always been a very dominant factor in world education. That group of twelve are working in every educational center in the world.

20. These groups are not an organization here or anywhere that makes propaganda for world peace.

It was seen that the spoken word, or the silent word, when sent out to the world, was of far greater influence than the written word. The written word can be garbled. The spoken word is an ever-expanding and ever-increasing influence.

21. Here again is the wisdom of the wise which has always been in evidence. So long as constructive forces work in "secret" they grow unnoticed by those who would destroy their effect. The world does not realize the advance of the Constructive Force until it has already undermined the sordid structures of the selfish and self-seeking and then it is too late. At the time of such helpless disintegration, and only then, are the activities of the Brotherhood likely to come out into the open to strengthen the Truth in the minds of all the people. This is not done through fear of attack but through knowledge of the most powerful way to bring about any great constructive movement for world betterment. The selfish have no access to it.

22. In a sense, all those who are working for India's freedom or for the freedom and peace of the world are Avatars, as the Western World looks at the Avatars. Many of the Great Ones have been disseminating this teaching for thousands of years. Jesus has been and is working definitely for the betterment of the whole world.

23. The reason many people in the Western World do not recognize the work of Avatars is that they can conceive of them only as working on the surface, saying and doing spectacular and miraculous things in public. They do not know that the true miracles are always worked out in silence first.

24. Regarding arbitration as an instrument for world peace, this movement was started in the Punjab of India. It is a powerful instrument of world

peace. It has completely outlawed aggression. India never did use an aggressive attitude, never did encourage open warfare in that territory at all, and the Punjab was the greatest influence back of this whole movement. It has been maintained throughout India for about three thousand years. Non-aggression and arbitration have been proved practical.

25. W. J. Bryan, consciously or unconsciously actuated by the silent influence, succeeded in getting peace treaties with all but four nations. So far no national character has since dared to take up his work. It will be taken up again some day in the future with the forming of a board of men, unknown to the outer world, that will have complete authority from the peace societies and groups working unselfishly for world peace.

26. If all the financial world were to get behind this movement for unity, it would be the greatest influence for peace. There could then be no finances for war. It could be impossible to finance war and hence there could be no war. If the cooperative system should be adopted universally, there could be no booms and no more depressions. It would also be of great influence in the abolition of war. As a matter of fact, cooperation is coming into existence. The people who do not cooperate and align themselves with the new order will be outlawed completely.

27. Following this spreading tendency to outlaw war, people will have their eyes opened to the causes of war, which are in the sole promotion of group or national advantages. The practice of non-cooperation will also be outlawed as a contributing cause of war. This brings the whole thing right down to the individual and each one must outlaw his own selfishness and self-seeking at the expense of others. He as an individual will find that the best way to promote his own interest is to promote the common in-

terest and the only way to preserve his own good is to preserve the good of the whole. This silent tendency is now being awakened on a broad scale. But each individual must find its beginning in himself and one who will earnestly search his own soul will find the embryo of this movement increasing in his own nature every day. Spreading from individual to individual it will grow into a mighty world movement and will be the ultimate motive in all human activities. Just as the individual who does not obey this eternal trend of his inner nature is destroyed, so will such groups, institutions, religious organizations, races and nations be disintegrated, leaving the world for those who love the law of God and live that law in relationship to every other man and nation.

28. In all modern movements it is clearly revealed that the changes must be first in the individual for, unless his own nature is properly correlated with the movement back of outer conduct, he becomes a disintegrating factor in any movement that might otherwise accomplish untold good. One can scarcely do anything in the way of accomplishing universal peace until he has found peace within his own nature and he cannot find peace in his own nature until he has been long enough truly in touch with the unseen forces which move toward the common good.

29. There is no question but that the individual first must be at peace. Not only that but he must realize what it means to the individual as well as to the nation. If he is centralized in that idea of peace, he projects that influence and he becomes one of the great moving factors of the spiritual development of the age. The peace movement is one of the most definite factors toward spiritual enlightenment as well.

30. Politics will be broken down completely with this new system that is coming. But, so long as the

present political set-up endures, no really effective program can be launched and carried to a successful conclusion. Everyone who keeps in step with the trend of the times is receiving all the help he is capable of receiving from these higher forces. Some of them receive this help consciously, some unconsciously, but nevertheless the help is there. Some have gone so far that they know and acknowledge this help.

31. Political parties, in the working out of the underneath movement of constructive forces, will probably merge into one great party for greater simplicity of government. These changes must come through our party system, moving into single chamber legislation and not divided. "A house divided against itself shall fall." That will eradicate a great many of our political evils. This will all originate within the States due to changes brought about there. It is coming as a national movement in the United States.

32. PEACE IS HERE! When we relate ourselves definitely to that Principle, it makes us a working unit.

FOR THE TEACHER

Paragraph 1. I should be clearly developed in the beginning of this study that the people generally need a new perspective in the matter of spiritual progress. We have for the most part been pursuing the whole subject as that of bearing entirely upon the body and the things which we imagine the body should have. In reality, all the body is and has depends upon something infinitely beyond these.

Paragraph 2. Show by further illustration, if possible, how the general reaction of the people is in the direction of peace and that back of this is the coming of the purpose of the Universe, or God.

16

Paragraph 3. Show your students how this peace movement which is springing up is identical with their own ideals, awakening them to the fact that they are inwardly actuated by Universal movements that are the objectives of all the illumined.

Paragraphs 4 to 12. Show how brotherhood comes into being through obedience to innermost impulses toward general betterment and that the difference between one's relationship to another in a sense of unity and the relationship of the White Brotherhood to the whole is but the difference in the degree to which they are actuated by these deeper impulses.

Paragraphs 13 and 14 doubtless will stand in your presentation much as they are unless your knowledge includes much that is only referred to lightly in these paragraphs.

Paragraph 15, 16. This should make clear why it is impossible for the average individual to understand why the Masters do not appear in the open with their work. Whole volumes could profitably be written along this line. It is the very reason that you sometimes do not venture to express your opinions even within your own home. You know as long as you are silent you have no opposition but once you have spoken the whole thing is open to controversy. Then again, you feel the right time comes to speak and it is all acceptable and everyone cooperates. What moves in the Universe also moves within man. To know himself in some of these most simple things is his key to great understanding and power.

Paragraphs 17 to 26. The motive is much the same and is but further emphasis upon the importance of silent cooperative work in the positive realization that the great Creative Spirit is working through all men in some degree; and the important thing so far as we are concerned is that we make it a more vital issue in our own lives.

Paragraphs 27 to 32 afford additional opportunity for amplification along the foregoing lines and can become a vital factor in liberating the people to progress. Teach the people to expect and prepare for changes. Become sensitive to the changes now moving underneath the political and economical structure. The change that will liberate is not in any of these outer forms but is in the hearts of men.

CHAPTER II

THE ONE MIND

1. We have evidence of the control of the One Mind. In every field of action we will note the One Mind control. Even upon this boat you will note that there is one head; consequently there is one control, with many activities under that control, and all these lesser activities emanate from that centralized authority.

2. It is only through this centralization of power and authority that there is anything like harmony in the operations of any organized section of society or even within the individual. We all know what happens when there is a division of power or rather an attempt to divide authority without consideration of some central motivating source. The orders which go forth from two sources to the various centers of activity can result only in confusion and chaos. If power emanates from more than one central directive head, the authority is destroyed and the entire structure is broken down.

3. Where there is one controlling element which has dominion, power, or control of motivating action, we are brought directly to that One Element and, thereby, brought to one-pointed action which we have discussed before many times. It is through that action that we do accomplish and that action brings us into a harmony with that central control in that we do not scatter our forces but work with the One Force, or power, which is complete control.

4. You always bring yourself into accord with that to which you have delegated power. That is, if you

believe in the power of the world and its environment, you are seemingly receiving directive control
from a thousand different sources and this is the
source of your confusion. You do not know whether
to obey the seeming demands made here, there, or
some other place and this division in the consciousness breaks down the entire structure of man's nature. He must know "Whom we have believed, and
become persuaded that He is able to keep that which
we have committed unto Him against that day."

5. That one control does exist for every human
being if he will but use it. Of course, the use of that
control must be conscious; it must be consciously directed or used for the purpose which we decree or
which we establish. It is through the establishment of
that control that our thoughts are brought into that
one power of action or one thought of expression.
There they cannot help but express that which they
send forth. In other words, the motivating principle
we determine must come into existence. "His servants are ye, to whom you yield yourselves servants
to obey," and the manifest results must be determined by the outworking of that motivating force
from which you receive your direction. The results
can be no greater than is the power vested in the
authority.

6. This central control of the Universe is often
called Principle as well as Mind. Principle does not
bind it as closely perhaps as the One Mind. Still,
that Principle controls and governs and it knows
what it is doing; it governs with intelligence, so it
must be a Mind Principle. The Hindoo always puts
it as Principle, or the All-Mighty, which means that
man does become that mighty, controlling element.
Man stands in his all-mightiness the moment he
projects his thought to that one control, that one
central directive authority.

7. It is all so simple if one looks at the entire situation with an open-minded and sane approach to it. You say in your own mind that this person or that condition has power to make you sad. This is delegating authority to a definite location or form. Obeying the authority which you have thus assigned, you embody in yourself the mental and emotional state which you recognize as existing in the nature of that authority. You could not possibly think of embodying joy from a source that you decree has only the power to make you sad. Then, through your obedience to the authority you embody the sadness which you have admitted it has power to manifest in you and you say "I am sad." You become that which you embody. This is the whole secret power but, to manifest that Mighty power that is ours, we must obey that source and embody the characteristics which it possesses; then we should not hesitate to proclaim "I am that," as the Hindoos put it, when *that* becomes the thing we have embodied. This will all become perfectly clear to anyone who will dwell on the matter for a time.

8. In this state will-power is not a method of control. Will-power gives us the impetus for bringing that control into existence but it is not the motivating factor back of the control. Will may differ entirely from control. Self-will never is able to project thoughts to one central point. Definite control or mind action is capable of carrying thoughts, feelings or actions to one central control, which is a definite attribute or element that man uses always and which he has dominion to work WITH. Not Over, but to work WITH. That is the very force which man brings into activity the moment he brings his thought to that focal point of Principle which activates all conditions.

9. Let us take a very simple illustration. Man has

21

power to bring his mind into subjection to the principle of mathematics but he does not have the will to make the principle act. The principle acts of itself and is a single center of control within its sphere. Man may bring his will up to the point of the activity of the principle but from then on the principle is the motivating force and through this subjection of his will — to be more accurate — he finds the secret of his mathematical power. The principle of the human will is that it is to be brought into subjectivity to some higher authority and thus man becomes the embodiment of it and is possessed of the power of this higher authority. Man's weakness is brought about through making himself subject to that which in reality has no power and this should be proof to him of the immense power which is possible to him. He must now learn to apply this principle of his own will and recognize power as existing only in the One Principle.

10. Our everyday life is a concrete application of this fact in that our statements conform to the One Principle or One Mind. We vision or project an ideal. Let us say that that ideal is for perfection. We immediately come into direct accord with the One Mind control or Principle. We project an ideal for ourselves to accomplish. If it is a high ideal that Power immediately becomes active and brings that ideal into existence. The moment that ideal is projected and the force back of it becomes active through it, that ideal is complete. That is, the moment the ideal is released from the activity of our will and is projected into the activity of the One Principle, it is a completed thing.

11. So long as there is any dual sense it is difficult for anyone to see how this can be true on the manifest plane. The Masters do not take into consideration any plane outside of the Spiritual — the Spiritual

made manifest. If we do not take into consideration any plane outside of the Spiritual, it must be in existence always after the statement is made, even before the statement is made. We quite evidently withhold from ourselves the accomplishment of our ideal because we look to three planes upon which it may manifest. It is found very conclusively today that it manifests only on one plane. It manifests on the Spiritual plane always. It is always fact.

12. Now if we hold to and remain within that Spiritual plane we would see it in its true expression. We would not need to look to the material at all for when we do we speak in terms of materializations and materialization is not spiritually a fact. The *actual* thing is the fact always. That is the Spiritual made manifest. Two plus two equals four in the mathematical principle, it equals four in the mind, and likewise in manifestation. This is not three planes but it is all the mathematical fact separated or differentiated at NO point whatever.

13. After the manifestation it is said that it does no harm to name it material or physical because you cannot harm the Fact. But it is always elevated or exalted to the Spiritual. That was Jesus' meaning when He said: "If ye exalt all things to Spirit they are in existence already." Evidently He had that very thing in mind when He gave the prayer: "Father, I thank you that you have heard me, and that you do hear me always." He knew fully that that which He saw as His ideal was already accomplished. To Him it came forth instantly. Then He gave the statement that "if you go forth into the vineyard it is ready for harvest."

14. Now, if we take that definite position, there is no question but that we would be out of all of this difficulty completely. He immediately rose above every difficulty by the very attitude that He took. It

was not a long, arduous process to Him. It was instantaneous. He saw completely through the nonexistence of them. That is not claiming that He denied them. It is quite evident that He never denied any condition. He always rose above it to the True Spiritual Condition and then there was no need for denial or for paying any attention to anything but the True Spiritual Condition. He said, "I live always in Spirit."

15. Our Bible says "I live always in *a* spirit," being an entirely wrong interpretation. The interpolation of "a" where it does not belong makes a lot of difference. That is where many mistakes were made in our understanding.

16. The Christian Bible says "God is *a* Spirit." The original was "God is Spirit," never confining him to one attribute to one condition. One writer said: "It is like trying to crowd God into the quart measure of our intellect." Spirit and Mind are synonymous. They are one and the same in vibratory influence. That which seems to make a difference is that we take our thoughts as indicating mind. Mind is consciousness, for mind and consciousness are inseparable. The element of consciousness is thought and when conscious of spiritual Fact there is no difference to us between mind and spirit. We are in a state of Spiritual Consciousness.

17. You are right in thinking of mind as consciousness in action but so is Spirit consciousness in action. They, too, are synonymous. Either may become quiescent or become submerged in the individual but they are not submerged in the outer condition. If the outer is like the inner, mind is never submerged in the individual but is only quiescent. The individual only thinks that it is submerged and to that person it may become non-existent because he is not conscious of it. The consciousness is always

there and springs into existence instantly if one projects consciousness toward that which always is, the Spiritual Fact.

18. The element of consciousness is the directive rather than the motivating agency of mind. Thus, it is indispensable in the sending forth of the emanations of mind or, as we put it, in stepping up the emanations of mind to their true state, providing the element of consciousness is true to the Spiritual Fact.

19. Today many scientists are approaching this same conclusion regarding the underlying cause of all things. They dissolve the whole structure of substance and resolve it all back to emanating energy identical with Spirit. Spirit is all-pervading; it manifests in everything. It is found that all elements, including radium, are reduced to that one primal element—emanating energy. But this energy, in the last analysis, is not blind force but intelligent force. It knows what it is doing. Scientists even admit that there is a certain form of "electricity" that seems to know what it is doing. This all-pervading, creative energy back of all things is aware of itself, aware of what it is doing, aware of how to do it, and we therefore call it Spirit or God. It is omnipresent, omnipotent, and omniscient as the Christian Bible puts it.

20. When man begins to assemble in his consciousness the activities of any principle, he begins to say "I am that." This is the centralizing of the authority of the principle in himself. "I am" renders the mind dynamic instead of letting it rest in potentiality. It becomes dynamic the moment we focus thought upon I AM. That focal point is the center always and from it emanates the authoritative commands that control and determine the entire status of manifest man. The I AM must be used to

indicate man's true estate, that which he is in fact, and not what he has seemed to himself to be in manifest form. "I am *THAT* I am," which is the embodiment of the motivating authority of the Universe. Beside THAT "I AM" there is no true existence but only delusion.

21. This name "I AM" was God to Moses. It has come down through the ages as "I AM." To the Hindoos it is AUM, which means the same. Likewise to the Aryans it is AUM. The Chinese use it as TAU.

22. The so-called "blind spots" in the ether common in our radio and scientific fields is in a sense symbolic of the blind spots in human consciousness. The radio beam crosses right through these non-magnetic fields as if they did not exist. Our layers of atmosphere, the concentric bands of atmospheric conditions, are in motion. In our earth they are stationary. When a non-magnetic field moves over a magnetic field of our concentric bands a vacuum-like condition is established. When a magnetic field passes over a non-magnetic field on the earth's surface it passes right through it and is lost. It is frequently more powerful at night than in the daytime. These non-magnetic fields are like the static states in human consciousness, more intense with greater darkness or ignorance. But the positive radiations of the Spiritual I AM, the declarations of that which man is in fact, penetrate through these static fields of his consciousness and it is as though they do not exist. The persistent declaration of Spiritual facts regarding man's nature and his place in the Universe eventually will eliminate all these static fields in human consciousness as well as in his affairs.

23. The One Mind is not constantly creating new ideas. It is manifesting Ideas that have been created from the beginning, for the One Mind is and always

has been Omniscient — all knowing. It has never been nor will it ever be more or less than ITSELF. It is all a process of reverberation. It is the same as our radio currents today. They are flooding back and forth or reverberating from one space to the other space. That is, from space to space as you might say.

24. Thought is, of course, the most potent of any radiations because it has control over the vibratory field of electricity and radio. In fact, both the vibratory field of electricity and of radio will impinge and reflect from the vibratory field of thought always. Radio follows a track in the atmosphere regardless of a conductor. It follows a true track or trend. It operates through the ether. But thought in this sense does not "travel" for thought is omnipresent. It is already there no matter to what point you refer. It is the impingement of thought upon the electrons that causes thought to appear to move. Mind is the motivating element, thought moving concurrently with mind and in striking upon the electrons produces all movement in the plane of manifest substances.

25. That which we call space is in reality the One Spiritual Mind. That is the Principle by which the human soul, which is the replica of the Spiritual mind, can overcome time and space, for there is no such thing as time and space in Spirit. In Spirit all is complete and in completeness there can be no such thing as time or space. This is what is meant by "letting the same mind be in you which was also in Christ." It is a state of complete oneness existing in fact between the individual and the Universal soul and it must become a conscious fact to the individual. That is the complete Mind, the controlling mind, functioning through the individual consciously.

26. Physical man or man conscious of himself only as a physical being that thinks he is apart from

God, the One Mind, and thinks in terms of moving from place to place, is only moving in illusion for himself and, hence, unhappiness. He really is in and of that One Mind and lives and moves and has his being in IT. In Jesus' talks His greatest statement was "Peace be still." It is never said in a loud voice, projected of the will of man, but in unison with the calm, knowing power that comes from a sense of Oneness. There is the greatest security and the greatest power. We have seen some of the greatest storms overcome by that simple statement. Likewise, the seeming "brain storms" of human mind are stilled until one can feel the controlling power of the One Mind.

FOR THE TEACHER

Paragraphs 1 and 2 give ample opportunity to conclusively point out to the individual that so long as his mind is divided he has, by that act of division, lost his sense of power and direction. Only from some definite premise can any structure be builded and until one has arrived at this premise he cannot proceed to do anything. This must have been what Jesus meant when he said, "Thou shalt worship the Lord thy God, and Him only shalt thou serve."

Paragraph 3. This one underlying principle of Life, God, is the controlling and ruling force of the Universe and man can find himself only in relationship to this principle. The only adjustment that will harmonize man's being is a realignment of his entire nature with the facts from which he came.

Paragraph 4. Man himself has assigned power to the external world for there is no power there originally, nor is power there even when he has seemed to delegate it. That power still remains within himself and that which seems to be power in environment or anything outside of his own I AM, his central identity, is the perversion of this same power within himself. The power is always within man and it works according to the direction given it. But back of it all is the controlling force of the Universe and that which I am individually must be one with the I AM which is universal. Perfect accord must exist between cause and effect for the movement of the cause is the life of the effect.

Paragraphs 5, 6 and 7 can be further extended along this same line and the lesson made of eternal benefit to every individual. Nothing else so completely tallies with the true message which Christ tried to give to the world as this. "Greater things than these shall ye do" was His estimate of man's potential capacity.

Paragraphs 8 and 9. The most helpful lesson and liberating practice can be developed from these two paragraphs. The willful attempt to force thought into the plane of manifestation is a hopeless task. It is destructive to the individual who practices it. The acceptance of Universal Power, a central executive emanation that produced heaven and earth as the already-completed manifestation of itself and the self-existent fact back of every constructive idea of man, is the way to liberation.

Paragraph 10 shows the method of procedure in so-called demonstration which is, in the last analysis, stepping aside from our sense of incompleteness and imperfection to accept the Facts.

Paragraph 11 shows more accurately what happens in this matter of manifest results. A freeing of the mind from all duality is the solution to the whole matter.

Paragraph 12 is a further extension of this same idea.

Paragraphs 13, 14 and 15 can be made to strengthen the foregoing.

Paragraph 16. Can we not once and for all make clear that the different "minds", as we call them, are but a difference in thought? Mind functioning as what we call mind is this same spiritual capacity in man functioning in its lowest capacity through perverting it to lesser purposes. When man "thinks the thoughts of God after him" his mind is then spiritualized or functioning in its true field with God thoughts, thinking as God thinks or, more accurately, knowing as God knows. The human mind thinks; the God Mind KNOWS.

Paragraphs 17, 18 and 19 give excellent opportunity to extend this idea further and to drive home the idea that man is not truly living until he consciously functions in harmony with his source.

Paragraphs 20 and 21. The true use of the "I AM" is to maintain man's original identity in and with his source, not allowing it to descend to include within his nature that which he is not. Man is not his experiences. He is what he IS. Experiences with that which seems less than himself should never be admitted into his estimate of himself. I am always that which "I AM IN SPIRIT," not what I seem to be in experience or what I have experienced in the world. No matter what I have gone through or seem to be going through, I still remain what I am in the original sense, the Image and Likeness of God.

Paragraph 22 shows the far reaching influence of spiritual fact as transcending all sense of limitation. Spirit takes no account of evil, of loss, lack, poverty, disease. These are but blind spots in human consciousness. To the mind that KNOWS there are no such things and it goes right on with that which it KNOWS and IS.

Paragraph 23. The mind which is God is the same yesterday and forever. That which seems to be a new idea to us is but our discovery of what always was.

Healing and so-called demonstrations are not bringing something into being but are an awakening to that state which has always prevailed in fact.

Paragraph 24. Power of thought, so-called, is not the power of thought. Thought is only a conveyor of power. Power is in Spirit and thought conveys or carries power only to the extent that it conforms to the standards and purposes moving in Spirit. "My words are spirit," said Jesus, meaning that his words accurately conformed to the Universal trend which he called the Will of God.

Paragraphs 25 and 26 present man as an integral part of infinite space and not an isolated being among isolated forms. "By one spirit are we baptized into one body." Finding our calm in this eternal unity of all things is our position of power where all contrary illusion is dissolved into the peace and tranquillity of illumination.

CHAPTER III

DUAL MIND

1. Many of the Western World look at duality instead of to the One Mind or Principle. That scatters the forces and one is not able to hold his mind in accord as when he sees but the One force or One Principle and himself and all things as integral parts of the One.

2. "Behold our God is One," say the Scriptures, and it is only in the preservation of this fundamental truth that man lives in harmony with his own nature. Man is not a separate being, projected away from his source, but is created within the image of God and like unto God. It is only in the *sense* of his isolation, which is the root of all unrighteousness, that he loses the beneficent influences of the Creative Cause, which are his by the natural order of things. In this sense of aloneness he has imagined all sorts of contrary actions to his well being and is often inclined to blame the Universal system for his misfortunes. In reality they are all of his own doings, for the Universe does not isolate him nor is it accountable for the difficulties that arise because of his own isolation. "Return unto me and I will return unto you, saith the Lord," is the offer of the ONE to him who will accept his rightful place in the divine order of the whole created scheme.

3. Duality is brought into existence through thought and action without regard to the whole. But, by reversing the dual thought or bringing the thoughts to One point of action, duality is eliminated completely. It is a well known fact that we cannot

accomplish with a dual purpose or even with a dual nature.

4. In reality there is not duality in nature. There is the positive and negative, good and evil, hot and cold, all the opposites, but the opposites, when related and brought together, bring the thought to one purpose, one action, one Principle. In connection with the opposites it is not necessary to recognize them as opposite or opposed. The essential recognition is the single purpose. Jesus always said that His greatest accomplishments were with the single attitude or steadfast purpose, as He related it. That steadfastness does bring us into unity where Principle exists always. That is where Principle is always immanent. Then, instead of duality, there is that "single eye" or single I AM.

5. Many Hindoos use the I, while many use the I AM. It is thought by some that that was where duality began to manifest first — between the I and the I AM — many believing that this practice involved two attitudes or purposes, where in reality, it is but one correlation or subjugation of everything to the One Purpose. There is no duality of Principle but the union of Principle in all things. They (the words "I AM") even pronounce the exact Principle or Truth. As they put it, the exaltation of the One principle allows it to work in that Principle conclusively. We do not see, either, the duality of nature and thus we do not recognize it. As duality has no recognition it becomes harmonized.

6. Summer and winter are not two things but phases of one Nature. Winter is as essential to the growth of vegetation as is summer and only depicts two phases of a single process. What we call evil contains the germ of good and, when looked through to behold the good, the sense of evil disappears and

there remains only the sense that all things are working together for good. The apparent evil surrounding conditions of poverty and pain that are shunned by human beings, if faced for the good within them, would vanish. Jesus taught that blindness was not an evil nor the result of evil but an opportunity to show forth the "glory of God." A problem is not foreign to the principle of mathematics nor is it an obstacle to one who wishes to become a mathematician. The problem is only a statement of certain conditions through which the principle may be applied to produce a desired result and is a means of growth to the individual who so faces it. Conditions in life that seem opposed to our highest good are but points of practice until we attain that strength of character to see and manifest only the perfection of the One. When life is seen in this way all unpleasantness vanishes and everything becomes a sort of practice game in which we see, live, move, and have being that the existing good may show forth in our own character and in our world. Nature then is harmonious. All is harmony. All is working under the influence of the One Purpose.

7. Just as the difference between a perfect chord and discord is apparent even to the novice, so is the individual able to know within himself that which is in harmony with the Universal Principle and that which is at variance with it. Any inharmonious condition in the nature of man is evidence that he is out of harmony with the natural order of things and the secret of his perfect progress is to always approach every condition in such a manner as to preserve his sense of inward calm. This is impossible so long as there exists any sense of separation from the innate good that runs through all things. Man's nature is eternally attuned to the good for he is the offspring

of God, and God is good. When one is conscious that his good is eternally and unvaryingly seeking to manifest itself in all things and in his own nature he is in harmony with himself and the Principle of his being. By working to uncover the good contained in every experience man is instantly in that state where that which to others seems evil becomes the source of his good.

8. Of course, with the relation of the opposites we find that we come to the same attitude. It is said that there may be many opposite manifestations but they are not opposed unless the individual allows the opposition. The individual must harmonize the opposites in his attitude toward them for, in reality, they are never out of harmony. When we come to that attitude where all is harmony, then we see the harmonious relation in all things as well as in ourselves. It becomes one simple attitude of complete harmony. Then there can be no discord. There can be no discord in life or in living. There can be no discord between the opposites for they have their perfect relationship to each other in Principle.

9. Many scientists, through their research today, are making the same statement: The only discord that exists is with the human or the individual and that discord is brought about by discordant thoughts. It is said today that the American people are the most discordant in their thinking. It is quite evident that this fact is brought about by the many attitudes of thought held by the numerous nationalities which are brought together here. These nationalities have not yet been fully assimilated. It is found, however, that the great assimilating process is going on very rapidly now.

10. The mathematical axiom that only things that are equal to the same thing are equal to each

other is, after all, the key to all harmony. It is only as the peoples of America become actuated by a common impulse that any semblance of harmony can be established. This is also true of the world generally, just as it is true of the individual. Only when all the forces involved in a single organism, or in many organisms, become animated by a single impulse and move in perfect unison toward a given objective is there complete harmony.

11. There is no question but that Jung in his work struck a very deep key in the attitude of harmony in relation to all things when he related his experience of going into a cave. In many portions of India the people retire to caves in order to become perfectly silent to work out a definite conclusion about certain determining factors. In every instance where these reports are available it is found that when they go to the place where they are perfectly silent to conditions around them they come into the greatest activity of life. They see further as they project their vision further. They see completely through the material or physical to what they say is that perfect condition wherein all activity is harmonious. Then that which they see as true universally is merely related to the world of things. It is not that the world is subjugated to the spiritual but merely related to its original state; and then the perfection of the spiritual world is immediately manifested. That activity, in harmonious accord, works perfectly under their guidance.

12. In reality this is the same procedure which all men follow in the application of any principle. It is first necessary to leave the outer forms—through which principle is expressed—alone until there is clear discernment of the movement of the principle involved. This movement of principle is then related

to the outer form and we have harmony and rhythm in music, correct answers to problems, perfect architectural structures, perfect paintings, and perfect statues. All these manifestations are brought about because of the individual's ability to identify himself with underlying reality and this reality is then brought forth through the form with the same beauty and harmony that is seen in principle.

13. Now these same people will tell you that it is not necessary for each individual to become as they are in order to get into that harmonious relation but that it can be brought about in the ordinary walks of life. They purposely take that attitude to find out what happens, to come to a definite conclusion. After that conclusion is reached they are able to teach others but they do not teach others to do as they have done. They teach that it may be made practical; that it is not necessary to spend long years in meditation to bring this about because they have found a shorter method or an easier way; that the instant you become silent you are one with harmony or accord. Thus, from that very moment you begin to progress; the attitude of thought changes from turmoil to harmony; strife is not evident; consequently you have raised your body's vibration to the vibration where strife does not exist.

14. If *one* is able to accomplish that condition, *all* can but all need not take the long and arduous way. Once a fact is revealed one needs but to accept that fact. The thought of the Masters is: We have gone through the process of making the discovery, we know what the determining factors are, and the rest of mankind need not make the discovery for themselves but may accept what has been revealed. Consequently, it is not necessary for the mass to sit in Samadhi. They express it by stating that one who

sits in Samadhi is able to teach others what he has discovered. All may go through the practice of Samadhi if they wish although it is unnecessary for this reason: Through accepting the conditions which have been revealed, that acceptance brings about a certain leveling influence, a certain vitalizing condition wherein one sees more readily. By beginning with the revealed knowledge one is more easily adjusted to the silence, or the harmonious conditions and facts about him. Therefore, by following the conclusions of those who have gone through the preliminary steps, he moves forward directly into the Samadhic state. Those who have gone through to this state are the way-showers or teachers. As they say, it is not necessary to follow the teacher step by step, because they have cleared the way. They have realized the condition which has then become general and the projection has opened the way for all.

15. This is the truth back of the vicarious atonement of Jesus. He, as the way-shower, explained that we are one with the Father even as He was one with the Father. We do not have to fight our way back to this state for He revealed it as an established fact. Our work is but to assume as being true what He proved as true. We do not have to prove that the sum of all the angles of a triangle is equal to two right angles after it has once been proved. When it is a revealed fact, all we have to do is accept it. If that were not true, each one would have to prove for himself every movement of mathematics, mechanics, art, etc. But, when others have proved these things, we vicariously enter into their labors, begin where they left off, and proceed to the next condition under that principle.

16. The larger the group or the greater the number of persons in a group, the greater the influence. The greater the influence the greater the impetus

always. Therefore, it is said that if a group of one hundred would sit in Samadhi, or complete silence, that influence created would suffice for thousands. Therefore, thousands would be elevated to a greater enlightenment by that one hundred.

17. This is where the Yogis play a very vital part. They purposely give up a certain portion of their lives to putting out that influence, especially the influence for body perfection. And it is often said that it is not necessary for all people to go through the system of Yoga to perfect the body because they have gone through and made that perfection possible for all. That is what was expressed when Jesus gave His life upon the cross. They, as well as Jesus, knew that they were not giving up their lives. They were giving that certain portion to a higher expression that all might see and follow. They became the way-showers or teachers. Therefore, the people who could progress would go further and in greater strides.

18. These are the reasons why it is said that it is not necessary to go through all the many stages of Yoga or Joga. Many accomplish these steps in just a few hours because added impetus is given by those who have given greater time to service and greater impetus for that service. There are certain select groups who are working along that line all the time. That influence can be picked up, as it is radiated out from different groups and different centers all of the time.

19. This influence is picked up on the spiritual plane just as radio music is picked up on the electrical plane. But, as radio music picked up from the electrical plane is heard and felt on the material and mental planes, so are these spiritual influences manifest upon every plane below, for it is all-inclusive. It is all a spiritual plane, One Universal Plane

working in perfect unison with itself when the individual awakens to see it as it truly is. The contact is made, not by seeking the masters or their influences, but by seeking the plane of harmonious thought and spiritual influence which permeates all time and space and in which they work.

20. A line may seemingly have two opposites but bring these opposites together and you have a circle and the opposites have thus disappeared. Extend the circle and you have a perfect sphere, which is complete, synchronized relationship of all elements. As Millikan says, "The Cosmic becomes the globe." Then you have completed the circle in every way and brought about perfect unity. The point becomes the line, the line becomes the circle, the circle becomes the globe. This is true of every line of thought and through the continual process of relating all things to the One instead of separating everything, the point of unity or oneness is established. This is One-pointedness.

21. When the individual attains concentration in thought, he enters the Samadhic condition and that is where he begins to accomplish—when he reaches that One-pointedness.

22. It should be remembered, however, that this concentration or One-pointedness is an expanded state of mind and not a contracted state. It comes through the principle of relating all things rather than through the mistaken idea of excluding anything. Samadhi permits the individual to see directly through to the whole, the Truth or Principle.

23. This eliminates what the Western World teaches about the conscious and subconscious minds. In reality there is but ONE MIND, and that, we could call the Superconscious. That is where you bring the conscious and subconscious into accord.

You are then conscious of the whole. It is complete consciousness. Then there is no division whatever and if we make no division we are in complete conscious accord.

24. The division of the mind into conscious, subconscious and so forth was first put forth as an assistance in teaching. Now, however, the reverse is true. We can best understand mind and progress consciously in spiritual unfoldment by thinking and working in terms of One Mind. The divisions were a part of the teaching of symbolism now past. It may have been a necessary classification in that period but the race has now worked through symbolism completely. We are accepting the completeness of all symbols. When we become One with that one attitude of thought, there is where we begin to accomplish.

25. I have talked with men of great achievement and find that they for the most part work with the One Mind, with the consciousness that everything is always here and always present. That has been their attitude. That very attitude is coming out so dominantly now that we will find it is going to change all of our economic system. If we could be wholly at one with that Mind there would be no cross-purposes. Consumption of energy would be 90 per cent less. That energy is rapidly and increasingly being used for higher and greater purposes instead of being dissipated in efforts to take away from the other fellow what he needs for himself. The truly Great never have to go out and take away from the other fellow in order to produce. With them everything that is here belongs to them and that which belongs to them they are free to use.

FOR THE TEACHER

Paragraphs 1 and 2. Every principle with which we deal begins from a definite premise and only through adherence to this basic premise is any structure possible. The reason man's life has seemingly gone into decay is that he has disregarded the basic fact of life. This basic fact of life is that the entire system of the Universe is one single unit and that man is an integral part of this system. He is in no sense separated from it and it is only his notion that he is an isolated being that has lost for him his rightful place and authority.

Paragraphs 3 and 4. In these paragraphs it can be clearly pointed out just how the sense of duality was developed and, thereby, we may learn how it may be overcome.

Paragraph 5 and 6. "I" in the individual is the first movement of his nature, the central point of his identity. "Am" is that which embodies, or embraces within the "I"—individual identity—whatever it encircles. The "I" is a positive assertion and the "Am" is the qualifying element. "I" is masculine and "Am" is the feminine principle. The "Am" brings forth into being whatever it embraces or conceives. The "Am" must become immaculate in its embracing power if man is to bring forth that which is in Spirit. "I," which is my identity in Spirit, "Am," that which embraces or embodies all that is in God, is the true use of these words. "I am THAT I am," which is the embodiment of God. I can never in reality be anything but THAT which it is in Spirit. "I am THAT I am, and beside me there is no other."

Paragraphs 7 and 8 afford a wonderful opportunity to show the necessity and advantage of completely harmonizing everything. It is impossible, of course, to harmonize everything with our own thought and notion but we can at least recognize that since a thing has being at all it must to some extent contain the elements of the whole. By seeing it in relationship to the whole and harmonizing it with the All, we at least escape the discord that arises in our own nature, and thereby preserve ourselves in our true relationship. "God moves in a mysterious way" and even though we do not see just how all things are working in ultimate harmony with the Universal pùrpose, it would not require a great stretch of the imagination to admit that it must be so because of the very nature of God.

Paragraph 9. There is no discord in the natural order of the Universe. All discord is our reaction to that which we imagine to be wrong or out of its rightful place. It is only to the degree that we are not in tune with things as they are in Fact that there is discord in our own nature. Discord is not without, it is within our own nature. To prevent this discord we must harmonize with the spiritual reality back of all appearances. The mixed thought of America is only symbolic of the mixed thought of the individual American mind and all will be harmonized as we progress toward a common goal.

Paragraph 10. Illustrative of paragraph 9.

Paragraphs 11 and 12 show clearly how harmony may be established. All who achieve let the world's thinking and doing alone and concern themselves with what ought to be done.

Paragraphs 13, 14 and 15 point out clearly the short cut to spiritual attainment and should be made clear enough to forever free the individual student from the idea that he must do a lot of overcoming before he can reach his spiritual estate. He must accept his spiritual estate as has been revealed by every illumined teacher since the beginning of time and this illumined state is in itself the overcoming.

Paragraphs 16 and 17 afford an excellent opportunity to point out the value of individual and group meditation upon spiritual things. This is the real ground work of any center or class movement and to neglect it is to lose sight of the most potent force in the building of a spiritual ministry and individual power for accomplishing the tasks of everyday life.

Paragraphs 18 and 19 are illustrative of the same facts brought out in paragraphs 13, 14 and 15.

Paragraphs 20 and 21 are illustrative of the principle of harmonization and can be exemplified profitably.

Paragraph 22. This paragraph should forever free the student from the idea that concentration is a state of mental fixity or focusing the mind on thoughts, ideas, pictures, or objects. Concentration is that expanded state of mind to take in the Oneness of all things rather than an attempt to exclude anything from the thought. It is a process of relating all things to the Source.

Paragraph 23 and 24. The so-called subconscious mind is but a reactionary phase of mind to intellectual thought that has cut off a person from the natural activity of Universal thought. There are no eddies in a stream unless the flow of direct current is impeded in some way and there is no subconscious mind, so called, when the stream of illuminating thought is uninterrupted. When one is in the stream of life as it is, there is only radiant consciousness of reality.

Paragraph 25 is illustrative and may be enlarged upon according to the knowledge of the instructor.

CHAPTER IV

BASIS OF COMING SOCIAL REORGANIZATION

1. In taking up this subject of social reorganization we will begin with Hawaii and the situation there. There is a great similarity in the thought of the Hawaiian people and our own, especially when brought about by experiences. You can take an Hawaiian anywhere in the ocean that you want and you cannot lose him. Never have they gone out in their canoes but that there was at least one man in each canoe who could tell where they were as though they had the best compass in the world in that canoe. It was the concern of the others to work the boat and his business to pilot it at all times. They have brought this capacity down through the ages with them.

2. At one time we took one of the Hawaiians out into the Atlantic ocean where he had never been before and discovered that this sense of direction was bred in him. We put this man in a boat with sailors who knew nothing of navigation and he directed them to the Cape Verde Islands hundreds of miles away. The Hawaiians keep quiet and find a solution readily. They use this quality very definitely.

3. The great inventive capacity of the American mind is the functioning of this same sense. The difference lies chiefly in the field into which it is directed. Also we are all making use of it to a much larger extent than we realize. When we know how we naturally function and then proceed to consciously work in harmony with ourselves, we will make much greater progress in every direction. Did

you ever note how you yourself very often function in certain ways through an inner sense, or hunch, or feeling and then all the reasons develop afterwards which show the whys and wherefores? Many people try to think it all out first, then they never do anything but think, for there is no apparent solution for anything until after it has been done. The feeling that it can be done, or that it should be done, or it were better so and so is the first activity of this sense and, if one would be still, the rest of the information would come, completing his whole plan of action. Then the intellectual explanation or the thoughts defining the process would be readily formulated. The reasoning mind, as we commonly know it, only travels over the same grounds it has previously been over, but reason is never complete until this other sense is taken into account. The new social order will come just as the inventor's ideas come. It will be a flash of revelation, so to speak, and then the mind may put it together and carry it out. Man's description for this new order will be complete only as it is in operation. Reason is descriptive but this other sense sees and goes beyond reason, opening the way for larger reason.

4. This is not a phase of the super-conscious as many style it nor is it a phase of the sub-conscious. It is the power to penetrate into either. With the Hawaiians it is a perfectly conscious thing. It is brought about by involution. It is presented to them and is worked out through them. When they used to go on foot around the islands, before they had transportation at all, they were drawn to places where they were needed. I have seen forty or fifty of them go across the island to find that some of their people were in trouble there. Sometimes their friends across the island would come to them. They

never missed in those things. They were in constant touch with each other all the time. I have inquired of them and they think nothing of it. They simply function that way because they have never been given the impression that it is anything but natural.

5. Were the interest of those on one side of the island centered wholly within themselves they would not be concerned about the needs of those on the other side. They are unified through common interests and are concerned with the welfare of those about them and it is this interest that makes them sensitive to needs outside their own circle or location. Where there is need among their fellows they draw this sense of need into themselves through the bond of sympathy which makes them one and the needs of one group become instantly known by another. Selfishness and self-interest separate us, isolate us from the rest of humanity, and this sense of separateness makes people immune to their needs, thus throwing the social structure out of balance. It is in this way that greater and greater needs develop in one group while greater and greater abundance develops in another and the whole social structure is thrown out of balance. This is where war and strife develop. Can you imagine two groups going to war, each striving to meet the needs of the other? "Nature abhors a vacuum" and just as violent storms occur because of extreme differences in atmospheric pressure, so do wars develop primarily from extremes in the human status.

6. This faculty of the Hawaiians is mostly memory going back to former generations. They have never been out of it. There are no barriers put up between them and their former lives. They say, "It isn't that we have lived in this spot all the time. We see all of these places at all times from one point.

We have never been separated from it. It is only necessary to become quiet and then we know where we want to go."

7. In a sense this is the same faculty of instinct which the animal uses but, just as the man is much higher form of being than the animal, so are all his faculties comparatively enlarged. In the animal it is instinct but in man it is very much extended in its capacity, call it intuition or spiritual discernment if you will. The animal has it only to an extent but the human goes right through. He can see just what he is going to accomplish. The animal returns over the same ground it has traveled but the human being can go to any position without going over the same ground.

8. It cannot be accurately determined to what extent this faculty leads the animal into new fields but we do know that it is the primary function of this faculty that has paved the way for human advancement in every field of human progress. The only difference between men of great achievement and those who remain in mediocrity is that the great pay little attention to what has been done and what obstacles or apparent reasons may stand in the way of achievement but devote themselves to contemplating what can or ought to be done. Those who allow their mental and emotional natures to recoil, refusing to let this sense reach out into the undiscovered, destroy their own capabilities and this keeps them always in the prison house of limitation. But it should be noted that prison is only the recoil or reflex of their own nature. Genius is that which goes on through conditions and circumstances and keeps eternally in the process of expansion and extension of achieving power.

9. The ability to use this sense for unlimited progress applies to everyone. It is not for the select

individual. It is for all to use. The Hawaiians are far more conscious than any others we know of, except the Polynesians. The latter will come to Hawaii on a visit from a distance of three thousand miles. The true Polynesian and Hawaiian are true Caucasian. It seems that this faculty runs more definitely in the true Caucasian race. If they do not submerge it by doubting its existence or allowing it to stop with apparent limitations, it seems to be greater always.

10. This is what Theodore Roosevelt encountered in Africa. It is evident also in Alaska and Siberia. When I went out in 1905 to take relief to Amundsen there was no evidence of a trail at all but, when we were within thirty or forty miles of that village, the villagers came out and met us, told us how many dogs and sleds we had and generally all about our party and its equipment.

11. One reason the Americans do not possess this faculty is becaue they have too many accommodations. We have just let it slip by and have not retained it consciously. Subconsciously or unconsciously the American has this faculty to a great extent. Most Americans have had the experience of it but hesitate to use it generally or to say anything about it.

12. The average American thinks it a sign of being a bit off if something is suggested for which there is no apparent reason. Such a feeling is the result of ignorance regarding the true capacities of the individual and the most vital means he has for any degree of achievement. It is his doubt of himself and his ability that holds him back. "If ye believe and doubt not, nothing shall be impossible to you," said Jesus. This faculty is the first requisite to sound reason, while the other processes of reason commonly relied upon as the only basis of intelligent reason are secondary. Great achievements have

been accomplished from realms beyond reason and the reasons appeared after. Sound reason is brought about by first looking clear through the limitations, catching the vision of the unapparent, yet entirely possible, and then building the other processes of reason as these facts are worked out. "To faith add knowledge" say the scriptures but most of us attempt to attain faith by first knowing all about a thing objectively.

13. Then, too, we let others do our thinking for us. We rely upon them to think everything out, to give it form, and then we rely upon the thing produced. The producer becomes more and more capable and the dependent one becomes more and more dependent. Emerson said as much when he referred to the fact that what we gain on one hand we lose on the other. We have watches but have lost the ability to tell the time of day ourselves. To neglect the development of self through dependence upon anything outside yourself is to weaken your own nature.

14. The Chaldean astronomers got their information on astronomy through the use of the intuitive faculty—or the power of the mind to penetrate through to fact. They would depend on this completely and then work out all theories. These ancient Chaldeans included the workings of this faculty in their history. It has always been in evidence. The influence is still in existence. If we want it we must become one with it. That is all.

15. This is the "eye of the soul" about which the Mystics wrote. Through it men have read and will continue to read the Akashic records. Through it we may perceive things happening at a distance or envision future events with the speed of light— 186,000 miles per second. It comes to us at times during an earthquake or other extremity. "Coming

events cast their shadows before them." Everything happens first on higher planes; then reflection occurs here. It functions in the Devachan period between consciousness and form. It is the two faces of the Gargoyle at the temple gate. Looking one way it admits limitation of delusion into the temple, man's being. Looking into the realm of Spirit it admits the freedom and power of illumination.

16. The Hawaiians possess a great natural insight into things and they prophesy and prognosticate. There is a certain group of Hawaiians who will get together and tune in impending influences. If they perceive an influence that is not of benefit, they turn it over to another group who work against it, and it never manifests. The Hindus say that one man can prophesy and another God-man can stop fulfillment of the prophecy.

17. In our experience with the Hawaiians we never found an instance where they had failed to stop a negative event that had been prophesied. It is claimed that they have stopped many invasions. The ones performing that duty would lay down a certain line and the enemy could not cross it. Many times this has been included in their legends. At times the enemy could not even land on their shores.

18. The Carnegie Institute experimented some time ago with a group of Indians in Arizona. This group laid down a certain line and none could cross it except in love. Two men tried to force their way across the line and both men lost their lives.

19. The unillumined make the mistake of thinking that prophecy is inevitable, that if a thing is set to happen it must happen. "Whether there be prophecies they shall fail," say the scriptures. Prophecy comes mostly from the established mental structure immediately surrounding the earth, being the pro-

jection of man's own limited thought. The faculty of perception directed into this field may sense the trend of this mental influence and what will likely be the outworking in the material plane. This belongs to the realm of false prophecy and it can all be set aside. The scriptures warn against false prophets who turn the attention of the people away from God. True prophecy is the result of keeping this sense directed to the plane of Spirit until the individual catches the trend of the Universal Law. The law of the Universe readily sets aside any accumulations to the contrary in the minds of individuals or races. It is accomplished as easily as shadows are dispelled by the light. The sun dispels the night, a single candle will banish darkness from a room; for light, whether small or great, has unlimited power over surrounding darkness whether it be large or small. Only a little illumination on the part of the individual can dispel any amount of negation, limitation, or false prophecy around him, for they are only vague shadows with no potency within them. Do not accept prophecies of destruction and calamity. Look into the realm of Spirit and they vanish.

20. There was a group of persons in the Hawaiian Islands who came there from Japan, bringing black magic with them. They claimed they could pray a person to death; but that group no longer exists. Before one can practice black magic or become an antichrist, he must first become versed in the powers of the Christ consciousness. He gets the Christ power and uses it erroneously. The outcome of such practice is self-destruction and, with the destruction of individuals given to the practice of the black art, the art passes with them.

21. The most painful, if not the quickest, method of self-destruction is the misuse of spiritual knowledge. The individual tempted to use this spiritual

knowledge to influence, control, or gain advantage over others should remember that every edict which goes forth from his own mind or mouth passes through his own being and becomes a fiat of power within his own nature, working upon himself exactly as he had intended it for another. That is what Christ meant when He said that the Kingdom of heaven is within you. Your being is a kingdom, subject to the rulership of what you yourself decree. Whether his decree is accepted by another makes little difference to the individual sending it forth. It is received and acted upon within his own kingdom and he is sure of the most complete results in his own being. The kingdom within the individual will be heavenly only when he sends forth decrees that come from the heavenly realms, the Spirit where all things move in harmony to promote the well-being and advancement of every individual on earth. "The gift is to the giver and comes back to him," whether it be good or ill. "As you give, so you receive."

22. One denomination of Rishis in India is able to perceive an event that is set to happen. If it be evil, another group immediately takes it up and it does not happen at all. That was true also of the Hebrew race in the past. They prevented many wars among their people in that way.

23. Many are using the same method in preventing accidents today. Many people never have an accident. We worked with a group of over seven hundred people in the United States that worked definitely to prevent accidents and in the three and one-half years we were with them there was never an accident in the group. That group has now been augmented until there are about 4,000 members today. They work quietly and are not publicly known.

24. Why should not man put all the forces of his

being to work in some good purpose? By keeping his perceptive faculty, or whatever else you may wish to name it, working in the spiritual realm where everything moves in harmony toward the complete good of every being, there would be a corresponding action developed in the minds of all people. Because they were all working in obedience to the power that works toward the good of all, they could not possibly say or do anything except that which was for the good of each other. In other words, through obedience to the Great Law there could be no conflict among individuals. There could be no wars, no accidents, nor any of the other things that make for misery in the ranks of human nature.

25. This capacity can be put to varied uses. There is the case of the world war veteran, DeJong, who was treated in the Letterman Hospital at San Francisco and who, though blind, demonstrated that he had received a higher illumination by driving a car through the streets of San Francisco and Los Angeles. This particular young man had developed the faculty before and this was simply his sudden awakening. This often happens.

26. The point is that, if it can be awakened, as has been proved in so many cases, the faculty is there. If there, it can be understood, rightly directed, and awakened to proper function. We must give attention to these things and proceed intelligently to uncover the latent possibilities within our own natures, if we would arrive at the plane of mastership. No one can do this for us but ourselves.

27. This involves complete emotional control more particularly than mental control. We must be brought to one-pointedness. When our forces are centered, it works positively. Jesus said "One-pointedness is God."

28. The entire matter of our social reorganization centers around a deeper perception. People must learn how to develop this faculty. That will be the social reorganization: knowing how to do the right thing at the right time. It will help now to hold the thought of right action always. We will come to the point where we will know that everything we do is the right thing to do at the right time. This is the substance of social functioning in the future.

FOR THE TEACHER

This lesson deals with the motive from which will develop the new social order to come through these changing times and which will be reverting to man's primal faculty of discerning the spiritual trend of affairs, rather than relying upon the intellectual standards and material values of the past. Our past experiences have dulled, in a sense, this spiritual faculty and it must now be resurrected if we are to attune ourselves to the movement of Universal Laws.

Paragraphs 1 and 2 show how the more primitive races, as we call them, have a sense superior in some ways to our own and show how in some ways they fare better than we fare.

Paragraph 3 shows in what field this faculty functions most clearly with us but it must be expanded along spiritual lines if we would make the best of our own possibilities and opportunities.

Paragraphs 4, 5. This faculty might be variously named but in mystical science it is what is called the "penetrative sense" or the ability to press or lead the mind out into new fields. When directed to its highest purpose it will lead us into spiritual values just as accurately as it has led us into the fields of inventive genius.

Paragraphs 6, 7 and 8 are self-explanatory but can be developed further from the knowledge of the instructor.

Paragraphs 9, 10 and 11 afford a good opportunity for showing clearly how the mind of man is clouded through too much concern with the realm of effects and how it may be clarified by re-direction back into the realm of causes.

Paragraph 12 should be self-explanatory but affords plenty of opportunity for enlargement. Paragraph 13 may be handled in the same manner.

Paragraph 14 reverts to the same category as paragraphs 1 and 2.

Paragraphs 15 and 16 bring out to some extent the possibilities of this faculty and the fields where it may normally function. More may be said upon what the faculty really is. In its simplest form it is that phase of the mind that looks back to see what we may have done yesterday or what we hope to do to-morrow . . . the simple act of attention. If it is toward form, we discover only the complications thereof but, if into Spirit, it expands in the realm of spiritual reality.

Paragraph 17 brings out some of the possibilities arising from its use. This can be greatly enlarged upon and made of immense value to the student if he will heed the advice therein. Paragraph 18 may be handled in this connection.

Paragraph 19. The point to be clearly brought out in this paragraph is that prophecy is not accurate when based on the mental and physical plane. What is thoroughly organized on the mental plane may transpire in the physical unless set aside by a direct application of spiritual authority. True prophecy is proclaiming the constructive results which follow the authoritative application of discovered spiritual movements.

Paragraph 20. The folly of misuse of spiritual power should be self-evident to anyone but it should be clearly impressed upon the mind of every individual as a measure of self-preservation. The habit developing in many metaphysical circles of mentally influencing others to do the will of another is black magic in its embryonic form and can only lead to chaos.

Paragraph 21 should be handled in connection with paragraph 20.

Paragraphs 22 and 23 may be handled as paragraph 19 and may be developed further according to the leading of the instructor.

Paragraph 24 is self-explanatory but affords practical opportunity for showing the basis of true cooperation in ushering in the new order of things. The true motive of the spiritual aspirant is in harmony with the Universal Motive which works alike for saint and sinner, rich or poor, bond or free, and in a common motive there can not be discord and strife, hence no war. "Things equal to the same thing are equal to each other" is the basis of Universal unity.

Paragraphs 25 and 26 give opportunity to impress upon each individual student the fact that no one ever has developed or expressed any so-called unusual powers but that the same potential power is resident within him and his business is to develop his own capacities if he would know the measure of his own soul.

Paragraph 27. A whole volume might be given on the necessity of self-control. It is as essential to individual power and progress as the organization and application of energy is essential to mechanical power. Without it there is no practical power to constructive purposes in either field.

Paragraph 28 can be amplified according to the ability of the instructor.

CHAPTER V

POWER OF THE SPOKEN WORD

1. The spoken word has a great power but there is one thing certain: we must select the words and then we must give them power. There is no power in a negative word unless we do select and give the word power. It does not of itself contain power. Power must be given to the word by the one who speaks it. Of course, as the Eastern Philosophy goes, the thought which precedes the word is more important. Consequently, the thought can be the motivating force behind the spoken word and in that way it adds power and, as the Masters put it, that word must go forth and create.

2. Now, if a word is spoken idly or without force of thought, it does not accomplish. By the selection of that word, the power given to it through thought cannot help but accomplish that very thing for which it is sent. That is why they claim such selectivity for the spoken word and that is why they say the spoken word is always selective.

3. That power which we put back of the word to accomplish must be the energy that we ourselves perceive. As they put it, not the energy which you give to the word but the energy for the accomplishment of that word is what you perceive.

4. Jesus said, "My words are spirit and they are life and they do accomplish that whereunto they are sent." Spirit is the creative cause in the universe and our words are potent only as this same spirit is seen as the operative force back of them. It is the activity of the force of nature that makes the seed grow for no seed has power within itself. It is a container or

vehicle of that force. So it is with words. The Scriptures say, "The word is a seed," and the power of Spirit acts upon words as nature does upon the seed. Our consciousness or awareness of Spirit is the focal point in this matter of the power of the word. Idle words are impotent and do not create, though they, in a sense, may add to the state of hypnosis. To fear negative words is to add to their hypnotic energies and it thereby adds to the influence of the negative word. The power of ignorant or idle words is only that they may intensify the hypnotic state of man's mind but they do not alter the creative cause in the least. The power of negative words is only the modernization of the old idea of the devil and is a direct violation of the fact that there is only the power of God. There is no power opposed to the ultimate good in the universal trend. That which seems to be opposition is in our own minds, which often work contrary to the divine purpose. The creative trend of the Universe or the will and purpose of God is to dissolve ignorance just as light dissolves darkness.

5. We have seen them—"them" used in this sense always refers to the Masters—put forth a word and what the word represented would come into existence immediately. There was no time element at all. In fact, there is no way of placing a time element upon the spoken word if the energy—Spirit—is in it. As they put it, a word spoken directly with the impetus of true thought behind it must create that very condition instantly. It is quite evident that the Western World looks upon a word as less potent. That is, a word may be spoken but, with no energy behind it, it loses its potency entirely. It is often said that this is why the Western World gets into such childish prattle. It fails to put the proper value upon its words.

6. Now, the thought which possesses the proper selectivity or which possesses the force that belongs to it, should always be given to the word, not to drive that word through will or the force of the will but to give that word the power which belongs to it. That of course is the power of the Spirit and this is included in our words only through highly selected thought, thought which corresponds to the creative purposes of the Universe. In that way the will, which has directive ability, sends the word forth but it is not the will that gives power to the spoken word. The will selects or enters into the selection of thought and the speaking of the word but the power is conceded or admitted through an enlarged consciousness of the presence and power of Spirit. But, when a word is selected for its meaning or its use, it is always selected in the frequency where it belongs and is placed there.

7. This should eliminate the fear which many have of negative words and at the same time should inspire the individual to a more intelligent selection of his words and how to put them to better use. "To think the thoughts of God after him" would be the essence of spiritual power for back of such words would be the very power that created the heavens and the earth. Man's words should always be an outlet for his own innate spiritual nature and a means of establishing this spiritual nature in his outer being. To speak only in harmony with the highest and most constructive ideals would be to speak with the greatest power and, in this way, that which seems the greatest improbability would become the most probable in that such words have the greater power. In other words, the more Godlike the thought, the realization, and the consciousness, the greater the power involved in the process.

8. As the Eastern Philosophers express it, you

could not be separated from Principle one iota if you would use selective words. Therefore, every word that is put out can be selective. Then you are not energizing a negative condition. You are only giving energy to that one conclusion.

9. The Hindu, or the Aryan always put it: "Man is the creator of words; therefore, man is the selector or he has dominion over those words and he selects or places words in existence which must operate or become potent." Now, in the measure that he uses this fact rightly, there is no way of connecting that power with negative words, as they put it. Consequently, negative words do not enter into or have any consideration from the individual who wishes to manifest forms. This thought of manifest form is always that condition brought into existence wherein man is able to create. That is where man has dominion over every word spoken. The Sanskrit language in one of its phases allows for that condition. There is in that the power to manifest. By that we mean that one position of the Sanskrit language allows only four positive words, or statements. That is, words that can be made into positive statements and from these there is no deviation.

10. Naturally, everyone asks what those four positive words are. They are always words which mean the positive declaration of facts. Each one can select them. Of course, the most positive word is the first word, God. Going back to the Principle, you would formulate your statement with that as a basis; you would formulate with that word whatever positive sentence you wished. Thereby is the power of the spoken word. Your key word is always the highest, or God. Then you select the words which accompany that for your positive declaration.

11. Just as all mathematical calculation springs from the Unit symbolized by the figure 1, so must

all words emanate from a single derivative, or principle. GOD IS and, because God is, I AM. Because God is life, I am life. Because God is intelligence, I am intelligence. Because God is power, I am power. Because God is all substance, I am substance, et cetera. Father in Sanskrit means first mover and the first movement of the mind of the individual must always emanate from the One Source and it must be sustained through the consciousness of the individual. To admit anything into the individual consciousness that does not originate in the facts of God is to adulterate the process of life in himself and, to this extent, he becomes unaware of the fullness of his Divinity. He must give himself to the underlying facts of life in their entirety; he must tarry at Jerusalem—his contact with The All—until the Holy, or entire spirit of God is the motivating energy of his every thought, word, and act.

12. Man cannot express a word or thought outside of his own field of competency with any manifesting power. He cannot go outside of that field because that very word which he expresses creates the field in which he acts.

13. The average person does not really know what a word is. It is merely a vehicle used in the processes of mind to convey or extend certain processes of the mind. The word cannot convey that which is not in the mind. Webster says that a "name" implies the "essential nature" of a thing. A word is only a name for certain states of consciousness and that is something that rests with the individual himself. One person may say "I am happy" and it would convey nothing to another individual hearing the word. If his consciousness is only a bit joyous, his words would convey but little authority.

But if he were radiant with joy his words would convey complete conviction. Idle words are empty words, words which do not contain the consciousness and realization of spiritual facts. You see, a word as we use it is just what it contains and the content of the word is determined by our consciousness and our consciousness is determined by the degree of intelligent selection which we use.

14. It is not repetition that makes a word effective. Your first declaration, if it be true, is sufficient. There is nothing left to do but stand by your statement, abide in your word. Repetition, however, is often an effective means of bringing one into accord with the possibilities contained within a statement. One often repeats a sentence or rule over and over before the meaning is clearly revealed to his consciousness. Without this expansion of the mind toward the inner facts repetition is only hypnotic.

15. If man repeats words and they do not become hypnotic to him, this repetition brings him into closer accord with the facts back of the words. It effects a higher realization. It is worth while to repeat up to a certain point and then it is not worth while even to repeat because your word is established unto you. When you understand that your word is clearly established repetition is of no more value whatever. In REALITY, we come to understand that our word is always established and we never repeat it.

16. If the manifestation of your word does not appear, that is no proof of its ineffectiveness. The better policy in such a case is to give thanks that the manifestation is there. You get out of doubt completely in that way. But, by going on and repeating your word, you may very quickly begin to engender

doubt; whereas, if you give thanks, you are more closely in harmony with your word and become more easily aware that your word is established.

17. The mere repetition of a word does not establish it any more firmly. It only brings you into harmony with that which IS. It is very often possible to bring yourself into more harmonious relationship by giving thanks that it is here NOW and that it is established.

18. When one realizes that the whole problem of manifest results is more a matter of opening up the consciousness to see or include something which already exists in Fact, instead of trying to bring something that is not out into manifest form, then the matter will be much simpler. It is "the land thou seest, that will I give unto thee as an inheritance," that contains all the mystery. It is a fact in Spirit, it is a fact everywhere and on all so-called planes, for there is only one plane and that is spiritual. As the mind expands to see or grasp the spiritual fact, there can be no question whatever about the manifestation of that fact. If it is so in God, it is so everywhere for God is all. It is all a matter of awareness upon our part and our awareness must be expanded to include the reality and existence of the Spiritual fact.

19. That was Jesus' method of working. Every word was established unto Him. He exalted every word through His exalted consciousness, knowing that it was already in existence. The Hindu stands in the same position. He states his declaration and then he may say that it is finished. He takes the attitude that it is already finished; it is already in existence; it is his; and then he goes on. One accomplishes far more in that way than to go back to the repetition and it seems to always make one stronger.

20. In the matter of treatment of so-called dis-

ease, the average metaphysician makes the mistake of dealing with the opposites, disease and health. Here are two conditions, the one to replace the other. In the East they do not work in this way any more than did Jesus. When you seek for perfection, know that it is established unto you. Exalt perfection. Perfection exists independent of both the opposites of health and disease. Perfection is an eternally established fact in principle and it is complete within itself on every so-called plane. Both health and disease are delusions according to Eastern Philosophy for they are only human concepts. For instance, your own idea of health today would not suffice you in five years from now for health is a relative idea in your own consciousness. There is nothing relative in Being, all is complete, all is perfect, and the true practitioner identifies himself with reality and does not deal with delusion. Let go of the opposites altogether and put in their place the perfection. We find that Jesus did not in any instance treat with the opposites. He put into the place of both the opposites the true perfection. His great statement was perfection always and that perfection was always established unto Him.

21. If I place on the blackboard the figures two plus two equals three and then follow with two plus two equals five, would you deal with the three and five and try to establish the right answer? No, you would go right through these figures, deal with the fact that two plus two equals four, and both these extremes would vanish. That which is less or more than the correct answer has nothing to do with the fact in Principle and it is only by bringing the fact of principle to bear upon the situation that any correct answer is possible. Our ideas of health and disease are both less than the perfection which is established in the foundations of the Universe and never

can that which is less than perfection be made into perfection. You are dealing with something unrelated to either of these extremes. "Be ye perfect, even as your Father in heaven is perfect," is the correct standard of procedure here.

22. Most people fail in the so-called demonstration because they make a statement of perfection and then immediately begin to look back into the matter of the opposites. Only "if thine eye be single shall thy body be filled with light." Lot's wife turned and saw double and her body became stone or salt. "Now, henceforth and forever, see only perfection," said Jesus. The moment that we establish perfection, the Christ stands forth dominant. Each works to establish the other, for the fact in Spirit is the form of its manifestation.

23. The effect of true spiritual treatment is not dependent upon the degree of unfoldment or spiritual development of the person "treated". We need not bother about his consciousness for it is based upon the opposites else he would not be ill. The spiritual Fact IS and the moment we stand in perfection our consciousness is perfect as well.

24. Speaking the Word is never hypnotic for it is the essence of the true nature of all creation. Treatment, or speaking the Word, is not projecting our ideas of health to offset disease. This latter is hypnotic. Speaking the Word is only telling the Truth, declaring that which always has been and always will be true of any individual, condition, or circumstance, in Principle. Hypnosis is a result of speaking from the human mind with its imperfect concepts.

25. It is not necessary that the sick or needy person ask for your help nor that he be conscious that you are sending forth the Word to him. If you send it forth on the Christ Right Ray, you are merely presenting his own innate perfection to him. In this

way you liberate both yourself and him for you are not dealing with anything but fact. You are not working against the will of any individual when you work with perfection for the innate will of everyone is for perfection. This rather frees his will from its entanglements in the realm of false habits and concepts. There is no so-called "Influence" in this sort of facing the situation. It is merely calling forth that which has always existed until it arrests the attention of everyone involved and they merely see that it is so.

26. There is power in the spoken word always if we see it as Spirit, for then it can be nothing but Spirit. We are the determinator. We are both the power and the expressor of that power and we are the sole determinator of what that word shall carry with it. There is power in medicine on exactly this same basis. It is but the conveyor or means by which the mind of the patient is expanded to admit the creative authority of the Universe. God is in the doctor, the patient, or the pill. Any individual, regardless of his profession or status, need only project the perfection. Of course, if we always would work in that perfection and manifestation of perfection we soon would get out of Medicine completely. Our Word would heal.

27. There is no harm in using an agency in an attempt to minister to the needs of suffering mankind. There are many steps and many methods but only one Power. If our ideal is Perfection, we are going to arrive at a point where there are no agencies. The agency which an individual employs only indicates the progress he has made in his own mind as to the suitable and most efficient means of admitting perfection into his being. One thinks it must come through a pill, one thinks it will come through affirmations, but, through whatever it comes, it is

the Perfection of Principle that manifests. Only the highest ideals are adequate to contain the full measure of power that exists in Divine Principle, for the larger the container the more can be conveyed. When the container and the contained are one—Perfection—then it is complete in every plane.

28. In treating at a distance, or what metaphysicians call absent treatment, thought is more rapid and potent than words. Thought does not know time and space while a word or audible sound belongs on the material plane and must traverse space and endure in time in order to reach its destination. Notice how instantly your thought is at the sun, the center of the earth, or at any other place. Thought does not travel, it is already there. Every fact in Spirit is already there and, further, it is already in evidence. To see this fact is to lift yourself into this fact and to see it for another is to lift him into it. I, if I be lifted up—if the perceptive faculty is lifted up to the plane of reality it draws all things into this realm. This is the true approach, rather than to try to lift anything or anybody into the perfect state. We might as well try to make energy out of earth by using a pick and shovel.

29. We know a man in India who walks through a storm just by the presentation of perfection of that storm. He will walk through a storm and never get wet. We have seen him stop fires and storms. Man himself is the Word of God if he abides in that Word. "If ye abide in my Word and my Word abides in you, then are you in me even as I am in you," is the truth of the whole thing. When Jesus sent his Word and healed the Centurion's daughter he did not send anything as we measure it in the three dimensional world. Jesus, or Christ, WAS the Word himself and there was not anything that was made but that which was made by the same Word.

Therefore, the Word which He "sent" did not traverse space, for the Word was there as the Truth of the Centurion's daughter, just as it was with Him. He simply announced a Universally True spiritual Fact and outer minds became awakened to this Fact.

30. "Our remedies oft in ourselves do lie
Which we ascribe to Heaven." — *Shakespeare.*

FOR THE TEACHER

Paragraph 1. Was not man given dominion over all things in the beginning? If that be the case, that same power is resident within man yet and all the seeming power which anything has over man is the working out of power which he himself has assigned to that thing. But, even though the power seems to emanate from the thing or from a person, the power is really within the individual for that is where its activity moves and is felt. To govern the action and reaction of his own nature, therefore, would be one of man's primal secrets of power. To keep one's nature always working in perfect accord with the Divine Ideal of perfection would be to have all power in Heaven and in earth.

Paragraphs 2, 3 and 4. It should be clear to everyone, though it seems not to be, that the words we speak are no more power than cylinders in an automobile engine are power. They are vehicles of energy and only the kind and degree of energy moving through them determines the power. When Jesus said, "My words are Spirit," he meant to convey that he was conscious that the moving force of God was moving through what he said or thought and it was this motivating energy which did the apparent healing. The assertion of fact is infinite in its potency in the face of that which is not fact. Follow this idea through with any illustration in the realm of truth and falsity, light and dark.

Paragraph 5. The important point in this paragraph is to make the student realize what tremendous opportunity he is losing in idle talk. His words might as well be conveying an infinite energy that would free him from his mediocrity if he would only proceed intelligently.

Paragraph 6 should be carefully considered and we should differentiate between the natural impetus of an accepted fact and the imposition of our wills to force a condition which we imagine to be better than the one already existing. The acceptance of a thing given never involves what we call a forceful will. Receiving an offered gift is infinitely more effective than to attempt to force one to give you something that is not already within his mind to give. Accepting a fact that is universally true involves no supreme assertion of the individual will. Perfection does not come from projecting our own ideas but from awakening to the knowledge that it is already the established order of things.

Paragraph 7. Clearly free the student from the notion that negative words have power. They are only a waste of time and add to the state of hypnosis. The higher the ideal, the more illumined is the idea, the more powerful it becomes. Your lightest word is your most illumined word.

Paragraph 8. Use right discrimination in the selection of words so they convey or project into the manifest world only that which conforms to your highest ideals.

Paragraph 9. Man's dominion is over himself. His being is supposed to be the Kingdom of Heaven. Only the law governing infinite space should govern his thoughts and feelings, his bodily and manifest conditions. His sphere of rulership is within himself, heavenly only when that rulership is exercised according to the facts of Principle.

Paragraph 10 and 11 show clearly the origin of all constructive thoughts and words and that the entire field of thought and action should be developed from this manner of procedure.

Paragraphs 12 and 13. Show what is in the Word that gives it power. Repetition versus realization.

Paragraphs 14, 15 and 16. The function of words or The Word is not to project something into being but it is to expand the mind of man until he sees that which has always been from the beginning. "Before Abraham was, I am," is just as true of every fact in Sprit as it was of Christ.

Paragraphs 17, 18 and 19 are a continuation of the same truth . . . training the mind to see through its veil of hypnotism, the veil in the temple, to see through to the other side where all things are already perfect and in evidence. It is all a matter of training the mind to SEE.

Paragraphs 20 and 21 contain practical advice not only for the metaphysician but also for the individual who wishes to help some friend in distress. So much of mental practice is purely hypnotic and only substitutes a condition that may be somewhat better for the condition that was already there. Why substitute one human state or conception for another when the Perfection of God himself is there waiting recognition?

Paragraph 22. To stand by the fact regardless of the consequences is the procedure. There can be no loss but the loss of our illusion and the gain is Truth itself, so why should we hesitate.

Paragraphs 23, 24, 25 and 26 are clearly enough defined and highly illuminating to everyone but they may be enlarged upon out of the richness of the instructor's mind.

Paragraph 27. The difference between the *conveyor* and the *thing conveyed* comprises all the difference with which we succeed in any kind of curative practice. "It is the Spirit that quickens," and the effectiveness of treatment is the amount of Spirit admitted in the practice.

Paragraphs 28 and 29 eliminate the idea that there is such a thing as absent treatment of disease for in Spirit there is no "absence". Spirit is present at all times and in all places the same and needs only recognition.

CHAPTER VI

CONSCIOUSNESS

1. Consciousness is man's state of awareness. It is the capacity of the mind to know and its knowing determines his capacities along all lines. Man may be aware of that which is true or he may develop in his mind a sense of awareness that has the semblance of reality but which is entirely false. The truth or falsity of his estate is, therefore, dependent upon his state of awareness or his consciousness.

2. Consciousness must be that which represents the highest attributes. It must be related to all high attributes. We carry our consciousness to God consciousness wherein we are aware of all things including ourselves in the highest state. That is the state where we see through all conditions and all circumstances. As the Masters say, the veil is then completely removed—the veil that hitherto seemed to exist between the mortal or physical and Spirit. There is no limitation here. The mortal and physical conceptions are abandoned completely for the true Spiritual.

3. This spiritual consciousness does not exclude sense activity. True sense activity is included in the highest consciousness always. Sense activity in its rightful function is true spiritual activity. The senses —so-called—act in a limited manner only when not under the right determining influence. When activated by the Spiritual facts the senses function properly and are then said to be opened.

4. The question is often asked in what state of consciousness is the individual when in trance. Trance is only a partial expression of sense activity.

73

We might just as well carry our consciousness to the true activity or completion always and, when this partial expression becomes one with true activity, we are never in trance and we are never under any destructive hypnotic condition.

5. This same fact applies to what we commonly classify as subdivisions of consciousness. One should not attempt to classify consciousness for it cannot be subdivided. It is ONE consciousness and in that state we cannot think in terms of divisions or separations. The subdivisions are illusions, the same as illusionary trance. They are so subtle that they can be very deceptive to one who is not using higher discrimination. It is so much easier to see it all as One. The subdivisions originated with man. Man saw the subdivisions as attributes when they are really not such at all.

6. The thought of most teachers is possibly for clarity in conveying the message but it is better for them always to make it One thing. Simplicity in the end is always the greatest clarity. The trouble with subdivisions is that they are almost always considered as attributes. It is better to keep our eye fixed on One. We get into negative conditions through using the subdivisions. They are nearly always symbolic and most of our symbols represent the subdivisions of consciousness. That is another reason why symbols no longer suffice. It is well known today that we have worked through symbolism. As the Masters say, we are in the pure light of day in consciousness. It becomes far simpler to have that consciousness, the complete Light, as our aim without any subdivisions whatever.

7. Take the matter of eating, digesting, assimilating, and the rebuilding of the body through the conversion of food into energy, muscle, bone, blood, teeth, hair, et cetera. Imagine that you

74

worked out a theory that each one of these is a separate function to be dealt with individually and that you had to determine with each meal just what portion of your food would be handled through each one of these particular functions and just when each would function in turn. How could you escape confusion? The fact is, you recognize it as one process with many phases and each one of these phases is a self-operative process within a single system. In a normal physical state there is not a single phase of the entire system that functions independently but every one of the various phases is but the working out of the single system.

8. The body is only a symbol of the soul or the man who lives within the body. That is, the body is a symbol of the workings of consciousness. To protect and determine that which enters into consciousness, which is through the control of one's attention, the entire system of consciousness is self-operative as a single system. There is not conscious, subconscious, superconscious but just one radiant living consciousness of reality. This is the state of complete freedom from symbols and therefore from hypnosis.

9. Some people become so interested in the psychic sense or the lower phases of consciousness that a complete earth life is given over to it to the extent that the true consciousness cannot manifest. The best solution is to simply let go of it and become one with the Whole. This is what Paul inferred when he said, "reckon ye yourself to be dead unto sin, but alive unto God." The difference is in clear knowing and influenced knowing. Clear vision is what clairvoyance intends to convey but the commonly accepted meaning of clairvoyance is partial or clouded viewing—seeing only in part.

10. There can be certain relative phenomena

brought into existence through clairvoyance and clairaudience, as practiced, or any of the five divisions of consciousness but they can never be or lead to the Whole. You see, they may become false and under a manifestation of these conditions we may get a false concept completely, which I usually refer to as a negative concept. When we stand one with the whole we cannot be either negative or false. It should be clear knowing of Truth itself. We cannot reach that state of Knowing or that One Consciousness through mediumship or any other form of hypnosis. All are distinctly detrimental to spiritual unfoldment.

11. In that high sense all senses become One. They all become One in perfect coordination. Our senses coordinate absolutely and every part and cell of our bodies coordinate and vibrate in unison. One great trouble with these other conditions is that we are likely to have one member of the body vibrating in the wrong field and then the new cells do not attach themselves properly to the organ to which they belong. Each cell that is created represents the organ to which it will attach itself. If one cell gets out of the vibratory field in which it belongs it may attach itself to the wrong organ and then you have a discordant condition.

12. This discord is often extremely intensified by the various occult methods of concentration upon the physical centers or organs. This practice only superimposes a hypnotic state more definitely into the manifest form and greater confusion results. In the first place, hypnosis is only a function of a partial consciousness, or a specialized consciousness in some particular form or direction. Therefore, the more diversified the field and departmental the consciousness, the more hypnotic it becomes. And to wilfully work in subdivisions and phases of con-

sciousness would be the most definitely hypnotic in influence. The attention should always be directed into the whole, into complete oneness, and then the distribution of vibratory energy is carried on through the mechanism of consciousness just as it is in the body. Then there is perfect synchronization or harmony throughout the entire organism.

13. The idea of an inner and an outer consciousness is also a phase of hypnosis for the theory imposes a sense of separation or division. There is in reality not an inner and an outer consciousness nor a personal consciousness and a universal one. When the Self becomes conscious in the outer it is only one attitude of consciousness and it is complete in every way and it is ONE in and with universal consciousness. I and my Father are ONE.

14. We are then not conscious of an inner for the inner and outer are one. The whole is always evident. If we see and project our vision or our Ideal, it is for that complete wholeness. The Masters call that being of "sound mind," or completely *sound* in consciousness. It is perfectly sound and whole. The body is perfectly sound and perfectly whole as well. The Knower and the thing known become One. Paul included that in his writings but it was never included in the translations. We can become the known as well as the Knower if we will complete the two and bring them together. The trouble is that we make a separation when in reality none exists.

15. The practice of denial as an effective means of liberation into this perfect state should also be intelligently considered in this light. Denial is supposed to erase from the mind or blot out of consciousness, hence out of man's being, an experience or process that is not true or that is seemingly opposed to his perfect state of completion or oneness.

77

But is the ordinary use of denial as practiced in our metaphysics an efficient means in bringing about this liberation? If the denial, as it is commonly used, produces the desired result, then well and good but, if not, let us find out what is back of it and what is the efficient practice involved.

16. Let us take a specific case of denial in its relationship to what is commonly considered the law of heredity. Denial is in no sense necessary. It has a tendency always to plunge one further into illusion because the denial keeps the mind fixed upon the condition and it is thereby more likely to intensify that condition. The mind naturally enlarges upon that condition toward which it is directed. The purpose is that the condition be eliminated entirely and, in order for this to be brought about, it must be put out of consideration altogether. It is not to be countenanced.

17. In reality there is no law of heredity. It is only a manifestation. It is not necessary to deny something that does not exist. You will find it far better to put perfection in the place of denial. You will get quicker results. Usually a denial holds it closer to the individual, whereas, by putting Perfection in the place of the denial, you realize that condition far more quickly. And it does not matter what the condition is. It has been shown by repeated experiments that it is far better to simply release the condition. Free it entirely through nonattention. Dismiss it. That was evidently Jesus' meaning when He said, "loose him and let him go."

18. There is neither race nor family heredity for the one presupposes the other. People may look alike but this is always because of some former close relationship or similarity of past experience and environment. There is an apparent chromosomatic

condition that shows processes of evolution running parallel but these processes are not in reality parallel processes or parallel evolutionary conditions. They do, of course, run parallel with the human race as well as with the animal kingdom but not with the same frequency by any means. It is a well known fact today that every frequency of the human body is above that of the animal frequency. The transmission of the acquired characteristics can be influenced through the thought but it can also be set aside through the reversal of thought.

19. It is a state of mind that causes the characteristics of form and similarity in form is due to the similarity of mental and emotional experiences of individuals in a group. Two people, not much alike in the beginning, through long association with each other and enduring the same general mental and emotional reactions ultimately develop similar characteristics. A man and a woman living together over a period of years, if they have sympathetic interests and mutual emotional reactions, begin to look alike. This is a reproduction of similar mental states.

20. Medical science today is quite reversing its former opinions regarding hereditary disease. When Jesus healed the epileptic the disciples wanted to know whether the man or his parents had sinned. This was His direct answer: "Neither this man nor his parents have sinned, unless you see the sin." It was only sin because of the thought of the parents or those surrounding him. In reality, the only sin connected with the condition was the sin of erroneous thinking.

21. The so-called law of Karma comes under the same category. It can be proved today that there is no debt of Karma, that the Soul does not bring any

of this through. Spiritual understanding takes no account of Karmic conditions or any imperfect condition. It is as foolish as to say that one must correct his mistakes in mathematics before he can study the rule. The fact is that the mistake is erased of itself when one applies himself to the rule. One's access to the rule is always direct no matter what his mistakes are and once the rule is known and followed there are no false results.

22. The leading and better Universities in India and, particularly, Dr. Bose of Calcutta University are making the statement today that there would be no appearance of what we call heredity if people would drop it out of their thought completely. Even with the plant heredity may be shown but it can be corrected by the thought of the people surrounding that plant.

23. That which is commonly accepted as inherited insanity is only a condition fastened upon the victims by other people. They are in parallel groups. It is an attraction and not an inheritance. Instead of accepting this theory of heredity, Paul's idea that we have an inheritance from God that is immutable and cannot be changed should be substituted. This is the effective denial of race heredity— the substitution of the true for the false, leaving the false entirely outside the range of our consideration. God has nothing to do with things that obsess the human mind and we, as sons of God, need not have.

24. Jesus said to call no man on earth your father for one is your Father which is in Heaven. This, then, is man's true line of inheritance and to get out of his mind these intervening mental processes he has but to return to the foundation fact of his being. In the beginning God created—that is, the beginning of all creation is in God. That does not

refer to time but to fact. With nothing in his thought between himself and his beginning there could be no other line of inheritance for nothing would have access to his being from any other source. Thought is always the determining factor and by returning always to his beginning, God, man always inherits through his own mind that which is FROM his beginning.

25. In the second chapter of Genesis we have a wrong translation that has done much toward our erroneous idea of sin and the matter of inheritance. It does not mean that man sinned and thereby became mortal and this mortality was handed on down to the rest of us. It did not intend to convey that the sin reversed man's nature but that the sin itself could have been reversed, that it could have been corrected. At that time it merely meant an error could be corrected. Jesus taught the remission of sin rather than its perpetuation with consequent results. Mistakes can be REVERSED is the teaching.

26. All the so-called human laws, or mental laws, belong in this category. They are all mistakes in that they do not define the true governing law of the Universe and all things therein. But they can be set aside at any time. They are denied by merely rejecting them in favor of the true law. Bose has proved that conclusively. He states that all so-called laws of heredity are only manifestations brought about by the thoughts of men and can be set completely aside at any time.

27. First, however, we must become one with the Christ Self. It takes a Christ consciousness to set these laws aside just as it takes true knowledge to set aside false beliefs. This Christ state must first be attained, or unfolded and, once in this state, there is, of course, nothing else.

28. Hypnosis may spring from two conditions, a partial state of consciousness or a false state of consciousness. A partial state of consciousness admits of certain capabilities and one feels limited or unable to go beyond that which his consciousness indicates. All restraint, or the sense of inability to accomplish, is only a state of partial hypnosis. The false state of consciousness is the notion that certain things are true which are not true at all. This is a state of complete ignorance of reality. It is a mental state built up of impressions that are entirely false, states of consciousness built up regarding something—if it can be so stated—that does not exist at all or, on the other hand, a set of impressions that are entirely false regarding a thing that in itself is entirely true.

29. This might be illustrated with the notion once held by man that the earth is flat. The hypnotic result was that men were held with certain restricted zones of activity, fearing to go beyond these restricted areas lest they should fall off the edges of the earth. That idea seems completely silly now that we know the earth is round. It was round all the time but the people were as limited in their activity as if the earth itself had actually been flat with a great chasm spreading beyond these edges. Adventurers who had another notion about the earth dared to venture beyond the limitations in which others lived and they sailed out across the chasm without any difficulty so far as they were concerned. To them the chasm did not exist nor did it exist in fact. However, the others knew they would fall into it. The manner in which the condition was met was not in overcoming the chasm for there was no such thing. It was simply a matter of sailing out beyond the limitations of opinions and it was found that no actual limitation existed at all. This is

exactly the manner in which the Masters meet every situation. "What appears exists not at all," they say. They are not hypnotized by the opinions held by the race nor conditions as they appear to the race, for they know Reality. Their determination is in the realm of facts and they traverse time and space just as Columbus sailed across the edges of the earth. There were no edges to the earth and there is no time or space to the Master. They are all illusions just as the flat earth with its edges was an illusion.

30. This is what Jesus meant when He said, "Get thee behind me, Satan," as it is translated. In reality He said "Get thee behind me, limitation," for there is no such thing. He put it out of the range of His consideration and conduct for in his illumined state there were no such things. He saw through the hypnotic spell, the veil in the temple, and lived wholly in reality.

31. In sleep the consciousnes becomes completely universal. It becomes Knowing, with all attributes alert. That is why we can often do in our sleep what we cannot do when awake. We submerge it because of our outer activities during the day. We go on in a great hurry during the day so that we become completely exhausted when night comes and our consciousness immediately floods back to the All-knowing condition, though we do not know it. We are not conscious of what is taking place. We should be just as conscious as in our so-called waking condition. Sleep allows that complete consciousness to come into function.

32. That is why psycho-analysis lays such stress on the dream state as being superior to the waking state when used rationally and in its right order. But the two—the sleeping and waking states— should be exactly the same. If we would turn our thoughts to this higher consciousness we would be in

that realm always. We would KNOW. The dream is more of a clairvoyant state of a very low order unless we do turn our minds to a higher condition or knowing state. If we do this our dreams are true always and are not something that has not actually happened to us at all. Dreams ordinarily are a mixture of the earthly and the higher experiences. If our thoughts were always of that higher condition, our dreams would correspond. Our days would be concluded the moment we went to sleep.

33. Some times when a man is up against a stone wall, so to speak, due to serious problems which he cannot seem to solve, his state of exhaustion appears to quiet the outer and very often the solution comes through. He has merely carried on the false practices of living until he has contracted his being as far as he can. It is just the same as if he had gone to sleep. The cessation of activity through exhaustion caused his mind to let go of the condition and then the solution came through.

34. The method of relaxation which the Masters use is to let go completely of any outer condition and always project their thoughts to a perfect activity. The physical, emotional, and mental must be stilled by directing the attention higher.

35. The difference between the ordinary dream and a nightmare is that in the nightmare you have the psychic phenomena in evidence becoming connected with an outer activity and always thus permitting anything to come in, the same as in psychism or mesmeric influence. I have seen people hypnotized and they were not themselves at all. They would act like monkeys or go about barking like dogs. This is quite similar to the nightmare.

36. When you are in the nightmare, it is possible to come out of it if you will think of what you would think if you were in the waking stage. A

patient has been known to cure himself entirely of extreme cases of nightmare by thinking while experiencing the nightmare, "Just what would I do if I were in the waking state?" He would have accomplished the same result more quickly had he thought what he would do were he in a perfect state of spiritual consciousness and would have raised himself nearer to that state. If he would ask himself what he would accomplish if he could see directly through to the Spiritual, it would become much simpler and more beneficial because it would be permanent. The breaking up of a nightmare becomes automatic if just before you go to sleep you declare that you are one with perfection. It has no chance to enter when you are in this state.

37. This same practice can be applied equally to the so-called waking state. All negative conditions and difficult problems can be corrected and solved every time by this method. You will find it very practical to ask yourself, when faced with problems or apparent negative conditions, what you would do if you were in Spiritual Consciousness. Get rid of the complexities of earthly living in this way. It is really just as simple as that.

38. To "be still and know that I am God" covers the case perfectly for that is the completion of it all. And that other phrase, "God is in His Holy Temple, let all the earth keep silent before God and rejoice," is equally applicable. And again, "In everlasting Joy all things have their birth."

39. Joy is the very highest state. It is the exaltation of Soul as physical pleasure is the exaltation of the body. But it is the true emotional state of man, born from his inner release into the truth of his being. It is only when we get out of that condition of Joy and Harmony that we begin to get separated from the Highest. You are going to hear a great

85

deal of that talk in the coming years in all theological schools. It is quite remarkable how that is now being brought about and how this change is manifesting even in the teaching of children to become harmonious and to let the turmoil around them go on as it pleases without becoming a part of it.

40. The moment you train children to react to constructive ideals and band together to promote harmony, developing the mass instinct in this way, you are destroying the very root of all unhappiness, misery, want, and war in the world. Our past method has been to develop the sense of strife. The moment that someone acted in a manner that aroused any resentment or resistance everyone else began to take on the same attitude and in this way we have been trained to develop the sense of strife. Only by reversing the process and getting back to the true state will we find our perfect social structure coming into the world.

FOR THE TEACHER

Paragraphs 1 and 2. To grow from the present state of awareness of himself as a material being and into the consciousness that he is a spiritual being contains the full secret of man's attainment. It is a structural change in consciousness that is to be considered for all the other changes which he has striven to effect are dependent upon it. It is merely a matter of being able to discern the difference between truth and falsity, between right knowledge and ignorance. To be aware of oneself as a spiritual being, offspring of an infinite spiritual system and one with all the powers and capacities within that spiritual system, is the very essence of attainment.

Paragraph 3. An awakened state does not do away with the outer man nor his so-called sense activities. They are lifted up and become outlets for his illumination instead of inlets for limited or false information.

Paragraph 4. Self-control and self-expression is the law of life and not the subjecting of oneself to control by outside forces or even by partial knowledge.

Paragraphs 5, 6 and 7. The consciousness becomes clouded always in partial actions of the mechanism of awareness. To be only partially aware in any so-called phase of the mind is not complete consciousness. The new psychology recognizes that the mind is and functions as a unit—that it is one process and not made up of many functions and processes. Consciousness is the function of the spiritual man, just as eating, digesting, assimilating are functions of his body, and the physical is but an outward replica of the spiritual. That is why the outer is always called the symbol.

Paragraphs 8, 9, 10. Pure knowing and pure being are the result of clairvoyance or clear vision, vision which sees through to the spiritual fact as it exists in the Divine Principle. "And he lifted his eyes unto heaven" is the practice that awakens pure vision or clear sight. What is commonly called clairvoyance is but the extension of the physical sense to see the movement of human ideas in the mental or psychic ethers. Only the radiance of Truth itself is the object of clear vision.

Paragraphs 11 and 12. To impose one idea upon the body in substitution for another, or to attempt with the mind to awaken bodily centers, is the most intense form of hypnosis for it is the wilful imposition of thought and becomes most binding. Did you ever notice how a living sense of joy functions equally and automatically over your entire being? No part of your being had to be stimulated to that state of joy. Imagine how long it would take you to become joyous if you had to proceed to concentrate upon each part of your body to awaken it to the state of joy and then proceed with each body center in this way until you finally became happy. Mental processes do not produce spirituality nor do they awaken the physical centers. Spiritual awakening immediately pervades the entire being of man and when the I is lifted up the entire man is lifted up with it.

Paragraphs 13 and 14 may be handled as above, with further development if desired.

Paragraphs 15 and 16. Denial is not a matter of dealing directly with negation but is the practice of ignoring it. The first function of the mind is attention and whatever occupies the attention develops through the mental process. Therefore, denial is putting the thing out of the range of consciousness. "Get thee behind me Satan" is putting all negation out of the realm of consideration. It is not even to be dealt with for it is but a shadow. Light is that which dispels the shadow and knowledge dispels ignorance.

Paragraphs 17, 18, 19, 20. All the so-called laws of the material world are only attempts to define the rule of behaviorism in the material system. But matter is not bound in obedience to any such laws but is always escaping beyond the so-called bounds of these laws and obeying something superior. The ultimate governing principle of matter is Spirit for all the Universe is a spiritual system. Heredity, so-called, is not the result of a law at all but is the result of imposition of false states of mind into the process of life. Heredity, so-called, is not a law but the result of counter-action to law. The law of the Spirit of Life is the true governing principle.

Paragraph 21. Karma is likewise the result of

counter-action to the law of the spirit of life. The fruits of the law are deliverance, illumination, perfection. Only so long as this law is kept from the individual consciousness is there even a semblance of Karma or the effect of some other influence. Overcoming Karma is not a matter of mastering and overcoming the results of our mistakes but correcting the mistakes. That is brought about through understanding and obeying the true law.

Paragraphs 22, 23 and 24 establish man's heritage as coming from the One Source, and not from the channels through which he passes. The stream is the flow of water descending from its source and not the banks between which it flows. It gathers water from its source but only mud from its banks.

Paragraphs 25, 26 and 27. The law of the spirit does not move to punish sin but to release man from the effects of his mistakes. The wrong procedure is to be corrected, not that man is supposed to endure the results of his error. Man's nature cannot be reversed for he always remains a spiritual being. He can only reverse his notion of himself. Instead of doing this, he should reverse his mistaken idea that he is a material being and retain the truth that he is a spiritual being created in the image and likeness of God.

Paragraphs 28 and 29. All consciousness that is limiting is hypnotic to that degree. Man is a free, omnipotent being, given power and dominion over all things from the beginning. The only limiting influence is the limitation of his own consciousness. To free the consciousness is to free the man.

Paragraph 30 is the continuation of the same idea.

The balance of the lesson is to emphasize that the important thing is to learn, whether when asleep or awake, to bridge this gap in consciousness wherein dwells all sense of human limitation. So long as we keep ourselves open at any point to anything less than the highest our nature is circumscribed just to that extent. One may just as well receive pure consciousness direct from the Source, as to receive partial knowledge from lesser planes. Why be always seeking the lesser when the greater is more easily available? Why not train ourselves and our children in the knowledge of realities and let the limitations and ignorance of the world alone?

CHAPTER VII

GOD

1. People generally are interested in the Masters' idea of God and the location of God. We shall, therefore, consider this idea in the present chapter. However, it will be impossible to consider their idea without including man for to them God and man are inseparable.

2. The Masters talk of God considerably but they consider It as One attribute of Being — Being as one attribute, or a single entity comprising the entire universal system, visible and invisible. The mind of man got its idea of God through superstition about God. Man saw then nothing but the graven image. It was then necessary to bring him back to the realization that he is God, there being no separation between the individual and the Universal; that man is an integral part of the whole and is identical in nature with the whole.

3. They teach that God is right within man always, just as Jesus Christ taught. That is always the attitude and thought of the illumined. Man is God. That statement, "I am God," is one of the most definite statements that man can use. We have never known them to give instructions in writing. But they do give oral instructions or oral talks. They do not call their talks instructions. They are simply stating facts which are obvious and they assume that the obvious should be known universally. Therefore, they do not teach, but merely confirm what all men instinctively know and which is universally true.

4. As a guide in individual progress they suggest

reading the Mahabharata, the Vedas, the Upanishads and the Gita. This reading is suggested as preparation for one who desires to take the real inner work and for concentration. A few verses at a time are best. They never suggest reading a whole book through. They often read but one sentence in a whole day. The instructions given in the Gita are steps toward the accomplishment of individual perception of what God really is and to really bring the individual into the consciousness of what it means.

5. No man will actually know God until he himself experiences the realization of God within himself. "NO man knoweth the things of God except the spirit of God which is in him reveal them." The preparatory work prior to the discovery of the inner or secret doctrine as it is sometimes called is the result of training the mind to grasp that which is within the statements for that is the inner work or inner doctrine. It is like studying to understand the meaning of a mathematical rule. The thought is that, when one has trained himself to gain the knowledge of the inner meaning of the teachings of the Gita or the Bible or any other Sacred book, he is then in position to make an inner search of himself to find the inner meaning of his own being. Man is not a physical organism, but that inner self living through a physical organism. The inner work is finding the Self which is the God-Self.

6. There are so many orthodox conceptions today that hold to the theory that God is made in the image and likeness of man instead of the truth that man is made in the image and likeness of God. But they think of man as physical rather than that which is back of the physical, the inner Self. Man is really the image and likeness of God.

7. If God is the sum of all things visible and invisible, the Infinite One, the image of God embraces all time and space for there is nothing but God. Man could only be created in or within His image for there could be no outside where man could be created. He subsists within the very image of God, as your thoughts exist within and live as an integral part of your mind. Not only is man created within this image of God or contained within the allness of God but he is made of the very essence of the God nature, like unto it. If the cause is God, the effect is God in manifestation. Cause and effect must be one. Can there be thought without mind and can there be mind without thought?

8. The union of every condition brings man right back to God. He does not need to attain. He is God. That is wholeness of Principle. The materiality of illusion is that which gets us into all kinds of difficulties and strife. In that complete unification of Principle in man we rise out of objectification entirely as we know objectification. There is a pure manifestation of God but it is not a material or limited objectification. It is a state of consciousness expression of all that Principle is. But there is not the slightest degree of separation or limitation. It is like a ray of light among innumerable rays of light, which altogether make the light that is universal, but each ray IS light.

9. The statement, "I am God," accompanied by the realization of what is truly involved in it will heal any condition instantly. If you realize it and see nothing but that Truth, only that Truth can manifest. In treating yourself or another you see and declare only the eternal Unity with God. That Light comes forth instantly for it is the true light and then we know that unity is in existence within ourselves

and within everybody else. It is all accomplished. That is the Christ Light, the Christ Principle.

10. This eliminates the theory that it is necessary to do any specific work on the glands, on body centers, upon the body itself, or to treat disease, as you state it. The physical will fall into line as soon as we realize that fundamental Unity. When this state is reached the glands and all bodily functions are stimulated until they become harmonious. Every atom of the body is stimulated and aroused to action in perfect coordination with the Spirit. It is the Spirit that quickens. You cannot raise the bodily action into accord with spirit by the processes of mind for the Spirit is above the mind as the heavens are high above the earth.

11. The ten commandments are not the objectified law of God at all. In them Moses tried to lay down a law for mental and moral conduct but there is no such conduct outside the law of the Spirit and the consciousness of the activity of Spirit must be discerned as the only governing law. The statement, "As you stand one with Law, you *will not*" do these things, was the original intent, but has been translated, "Thou shalt not." If you are within the law of harmony you will not produce discords but to merely refrain from producing discords does not place you within the law of harmony. To refrain from discord merely involves doing nothing at all and surely this never would produce a musician nor would it express harmony. The active doing of the law produces effects commensurate with the law. Life is active, dynamic and not static. It is DOING TRUTH, not merely refraining from that which is not truth.

12. If you are in obedience to the Law itself you will automatically refrain from doing certain things

which are not included in the natural operations of the law. You do not do these thing if you follow the law, but in omitting these things you may not fulfill the law at all but only obey your own notions. "Thou shalt not," was the Mosaic law as Moses gave it out. These were the emanations of the Sephiroth or the Tree of Life. He veiled that fact and objectified it for the people but gave the Priests the real meaning in the Talmud.

13. When God spoke to Moses in a "loud voice" as it is given, it was not intended to convey the fact that He spoke with much noise. God is a "sound voice," which brings light into expression. That was Moses' statement. A "Sound Voice," not a "voice of sound." There is an important difference. If we have a "sound voice" that voice is One and will bring light into existence. It gives us that power. It may be out of noise completely or what we would designate as soundless. And that is what we are coming to today, the Soundlessness of sound. Then it is beyond noise completely and you pay no attention to noise because you are in Sound Voice or definite principle.

14. Soundness is wholeness and, when God spoke in a sound voice, He spoke in the completeness of Himself. It is like we often say of a person, "He put his whole self into what he said." It is only when the entire nature is aroused and operative that the voice is sound or that we speak with soundness. We do not speak partially or in any separateness but in complete oneness. When God said to Moses, "I am that I am and beside me there is no other," He was speaking in a "sound voice," for He excluded nothing from His proclamation but moved as a complete Unit. This is particularly illuminating regarding the discarded psychological idea that the

mind is a sectional or departmental thing made up of many operations. This is the hypnotism of unsoundness. The more differentiated, the more unsound becomes the mind. Study some of the people who are given to this departmental function of the mind, concentrating here and there and moving their minds about one section at a time. They are extremely unsound and are never safe within themselves nor are they safe to follow for they lead only into confusion. It may be a good way to build up a large following for a group of people who are unsound mentally are easily herded into organizations, but this ultimately becomes the greatest bondage, particularly to the one who thus deceives the people. Soundness is wholeness — Oneness. "I am God," spoken in the consciousness that you are one with the All and that the All is centered within you and that you move with and are included in the operations of the whole, is the only truly sound statement for it is complete. No structure is stable unless it becomes a unit and no man is stable until he is a complete unit in and with the Principle.

15. We cannot stop in our progress with organizations and systems either orthodox or metaphysical for they are sectional, sectarian, and teach a doctrine that is more or less involved with the idea of separations. They are only steps in the process of man's discovery of himself. We cannot stop at any point without becoming orthodox. That prevents further progress until we break away.

16. That is where so many people become mixed in affirmations and denials. Of course, many modern thought organizations become mixed up in that very thing when they begin to deny. They fasten to themselves a condition which does not exist and then, when they feel this false influence of their own mental reaction, they call it malicious-animal-mag-

netism. They begin to get into psychic influences again, being held there by their repetitions.

17. One is really not working properly when he denies. Denial separates us from Spirit for we stop to consider something that we designate as "not spirit." In Spirit there is no separation and, consequently, it is only man's separation through which he becomes involved in the psychic or phenomenal. Moses classified anything and everything in phenomena as a separation from Spirit. The orthodox churches evidently get into trouble because they allow a separation. They have built up a great image in the heavens, calling it God. There is a psychic determination there which they see, believing that this image talked to them instead of which it was their own voice talking to them through psychic influences. The voice of God speaks within man as Jesus taught. It is the Father within.

18. Christ's denial of limitation — Satan — was not a declaration of his non-existence but a simple letting go of the idea which was entirely false. He did not reckon with it at all.

19. Moses, in referring to the dividing of Heaven and Earth, evidently meant that the earth was the outer. In the Sanskrit there is a word which defines the Earth as the outer condition. That condition is to be overcome and that overcoming is in thought only. Moses meant to convey that Heaven and Earth should be complete and One always. He let go of Earth completely and then the One attitude of Principle stood forth. He knew fully that the form was a complete embodiment of Spirit as life.

20. That is what Job was trying to bring out when he said, "Yet in my flesh shall I see God." It even is expressed that way in the Upanishads. In everything bring forth the Christ Self and see reality in place of a differentiated physical body. The body

is radiant and pure spiritual substance and it will show forth this condition when the thought of its materiality is withdrawn and gives place to the truth that flesh in its true state is the radiant light of God through which and in which God is manifest in His spiritual perfection.

21. Flesh does not need to be spiritualized; it is already spirit in manifestation, just as water is oxygen and hydrogen in manifest form. The water is one in and with its source and is identical in nature with its source. To separate oxygen and hydrogen from water would be to disintegrate the water itself. "Your body is the temple of the living God" in exactly the same manner and, when reunited with its source, the body becomes pure and perfect as radiant light, the Light that was in the beginning and out of which all things were formed. That which makes the body appear to be something else is the clouded mentality that has imposed itself between the flesh and its true source. The body— Temple of the living God—has become a den of thieves, robbing the body of its true sustaining principle.

22. In the Lord's Prayer, "Our Father which art in Heaven" was not intended to convey the idea that heaven was elsewhere. Jesus meant what the original Sanskrit intended to convey, the everywhere-present inner peace and harmony. That is Heaven in its true meaning. The Kingdom of Heaven is among you. There is an inner meaning in the Lord's Prayer which cannot be given out except privately and orally. If man understood this inner meaning he would be in the Kingdom of Heaven. This involves completely surrendering what we have called the self and accepting the Self that is the only reality, which is the spiritual Self, for there is no other Self. Those who have attained follow this path and

enter into that which exalts the whole into Spirit. Such an one knows himself as God.

23. This is difficult for many to understand for they think of themselves only in terms of their conscious thought. All such thoughts must be discarded. The realization includes the conscious mind when the Christ mind has become the complete consciousness of the individual, for the conscious mind is then included in complete consciousness. All thoughts that we have embraced within our consciousness that are at variance with the Truth must be given up. That is what Christ meant when He said to "deny thyself." Give up your own estimate of yourself and accept yourself as you are in complete relationship to the whole. It is forsaking all conditions which appear outwardly in favor of the architectural design back of it all. The Christ mind is the God mind always.

24. When any individual attains to true knowledge of God his works will be completed instantly. If he would stand completely one with God, it would be finished instantly. Jesus said, "It is finished," and from then on went right on to other accomplishments. If we ourselves recognize perfection we become that perfection Itself. We need no other recognition. It is all God if we wish to put it that way.

25. That was the only thing which the people two thousand years ago had against Christ. They thought it "blasphemy" that He should consider Himself as God for their state of hypnosis could not fathom the mystery of His position, which is the true position of all men. But that was the only thing they had against Him. When we make that same statement before unilluminated people, those steeped in ignorance regarding the true state of all creation, they accuse us of blasphemy today just as they did

Christ two thousand years ago. But why should we care? So long as we care what people think, just so long will we keep ourselves in subjection to the hypnotic spell of the earth. But one who is awakened never goes about making such outward statements to the profane world. One meaning of I am God is "I am silent."

26. The attempt to make God a trinity came through the idea of differentiation of the One. The reduction of all elements to the One element, or emanating energy, leads to the three in one or unity and directly to the true Trinity or Triad as one attribute of Being. This is the Holy Spirit, the Whole I, the Creative Spirit as complete action. The moment we project our thought to the Holy Ghost we are projecting our being to the complete Creative Spirit in action. It is the movement of the whole as a UNIT. When the Holy Spirit comes upon you, you are conscious that all action within and without is but the complete action of the Principle in its entirety without the slightest sense of separation or deviation. It is ONE action.

27. There can be no actual sin against the Holy Ghost. In the original text we find nothing about the expiation of sin. Man alone commits what he himself calls sin and man alone forgives sin. The son of man on earth has power to forgive sin. There could be no sin against the Holy Ghost for it is impossible for man to divide the indivisible or to actually separate the uni-action of the One. He only seems to do so. That is where the Divine Right of Kings comes from. If the King is in his Divine Right he can make no mistakes and man, as the King, could make no mistakes. This did not refer only to a certain king or family ruling over a nation but to man ruling over himself. When he rules over him-

self he becomes a King. Every man is a King when he knows himself as God and exercises his God Authority to completely subject every phase of himself to the One idea.

28. The interpretation of God speaking to individuals or groups of people as designating only that particular person or group is false. What God speaks to one man or one nation He speaks to all men and all nations, for He created of one blood all nations of men and He is no respecter of persons. But, from this false interpretation man has built up the idea of a racial or national God. This has resulted in religious wars and built up separate groups into nations. The orthodox churches, according to Dr. Lyman Abbot, have done more toward the retrogression of civilizations than any other influence because of their hatreds. The first intention in the presentation of God was that you look immediately to the Light which emanates from your own being and from the being of every individual as being ONE and the same light and that God equally manifests Himself to and through all beings in exactly the same sense without partiality or distinction. The moment you can project your vision to that light you are at once conscious completely, namely, in the Divine Consciousness, and there can be no separation there. With no sense of separation there can be no separation in creed or race or nation and hence, no strife or war.

29. Referring to the incident mentioned in *The Life and Teaching of the Masters of the Far East* where Emil separated the jackals that were fighting over the carcass of an animal, Emil said, "It is not the self that you see, but only the God-Self that does the work." He meant to convey that when you get away from the fear of the animal and project the

God-Self there is peace and harmony. And they came together and ate their meal in perfect harmony instead of fighting.

30. This is the theory back of our experience in walking through fire. The Masters told us afterward that we had raised our vibration to such an extent that there was no conflict between us and the fire. There was perfect harmony and oneness. We clearly saw the fire raging all around us but we felt no heat or discomfort. Our clothes were not even scorched. This experience has quite recently been duplicated in London by a young Hindoo Yogi under the severest scientific test conditions. Pictures of this incident were shown in America on one of the news reels and Edwin C. Hill, famous news commentator, wrote at some length upon the subject. Copies of this comment were mailed to 100 teachers conducting classes on these lessons.

31. The life of the Masters is simply the God life. They always put it, "Life is Light." "The moment we express Light, life emanates." If you live the Life, then you will Know and that knowing is complete. It is not a life of asceticism or apartness. It is a Life and Light in unity, in wholeness.

32. Anyone may break his seeming bondage to a condition that is not Godly by simply letting go of the bondage completely. That was our training from boyhood on. If a discordant condition came into our surroundings we let go of it completely. The Masters sometimes go for hundreds of days without eating. They are not bound in any way. But when they do not eat outwardly they do feed upon the Prana or spiritual substance that is all about them. They take in Pranic substance and it is assimilated for the direct and complete sustenance of the body. Plants feed upon Prana and when man uses the vegetables for food he takes in Prana also. He

can take it directly even more readily than the plants and vegetables do, if he will.

33. It would not be the part of wisdom for the Western world to discard the Bible in favor of the Bhagavad Gita. Our Bible is of greater importance to the Western world for we do not understand the Bhagavad Gita. The latter is best, however, for the East. The West could with profit read the Bhagavad Gita, as it would obviate the necessity of wading through the folklore and mistranslations of the Bible. The Bhagavad Gita has taken all that out. The Vedanta Philosophy in most instances is the best exposition of the teachings of the Masters. Many people get a more simplified thought and can assimilate these thoughts through the Vedas. Then they can go on to the Vedantic teachings.

34. The reason those of the West have difficulty in understanding spiritual things is that the Western consciousness has always been an evasion of Principle for the reason that they did not know what Principle meant. They even misled themselves, largely by the acceptance of their philosophers' teaching that Principle is an unknown quantity. The Master Mind knows what Principle is but so can we accept Principle and know what it means. We must accept the Goal toward which we are working or we do not work at all.

35. You cannot go into India with a Spirit of egotism, selfishness and design and get anything out of India any more than you can in these states get anything from these lessons, from the Bible, or any other source of Truth. There is nothing in Truth compatible with these attitudes. You get out of India whatever you take to India. It is not a matter of going into India at all. It is an ever present state is you can receive it.

36. It is not a matter of going to India, studying

the Bible, or the Bhagavad Gita. It is letting go of all these confusions that infest the mind and the upset conditions resulting therefrom. Then one may get a great spiritual uplift from the Bible or any other source. We are beginning to see that we take from the Bible what we take to the Bible. The very determination to get the very meaning out of the book will open its secrets to us to some extent. If we read the Bhagavad Gita or any other book we must take the same attitude toward it. There is, of course, nothing in the Bible that is not interpreted in the Bhagavad Gita, the Mahabharata, and the Vedas. That is where all the knowledge that is contained in the Bible came from.

FOR THE TEACHER

Paragraphs 1 and 2. Perhaps the hardest thing for the average individual is to realize that God is the great Universal Scheme of creation and the point should be emphasized by the teacher and practiced by the student until this very fundamental fact in life has become a matter of individual realization. Personality is an individual identity, while God is the Universal identity, the Universe as a single conscious identity, the sum of consciousness, power, love, life, and substance.

Paragraph 3. Man cannot escape the ultimate Unity that exists between himself and the Universal system for he is a part of that system. If a product of the Universal system, he must contain the potentialities of the Universe and, by whatever name he designates the Universe, he must also bear that name as well as its nature. One ray of light is just as truly light as a dozen of them, a million, a billion or all of them.

Paragraphs 4 and 5. It is not what man studies

but how he studies that is the secret of illumination; not what we know *about* a thing but *what* we know *of* it that makes the difference. As well try to classify and describe the size, shape, color, and density of seeds in an attempt to know Nature as to merely read the descriptions of God in the hope of knowing God. To know nature is to know it in its fullness, to see its growth on every hand, and to sense in some degree the force which produces it. Man must be still and know God in the same way; cease from descriptions and come to "feel after Him," if he would know the nearness, the power, the wisdom and substance that is ever moving within his own nature. This is the inner or secret doctrine.

Paragraphs 6 and 7. The same as paragraphs 4 and 5.

Paragraphs 8, 9 and 10. If God is ALL and man is created in His image and likeness, in what manner can man grow except in the enlargement of his consciousness to comprehend the greatness of his created state. He truly does not attain to anything but only in the discovery of that which already is. The point is whether he shall discover himself a little at a time or whether he shall discover the ultimate fact from the beginning. The wise of all ages have declared that the latter is the true way. "Know ye not that we are Gods and Sons of the Most High," is calling man back to his beginning, which is his perfection in and with God.

Paragraphs 11 and 12. If man is in a certain state of consciousness, he automatically does not express that which is its opposite. On the other hand, the elimination of certain modes of conduct does not produce an opposite state of consciousness. Action, and not inaction, is productive of results. It may be well, in a state of ignorance of the Truth, to refrain from error states of procedure but it is not this practice that leads to illumination. If you are not happy, you do not become so by merely refusing to act unhappy. If you are happy, on the other hand, you do not act nor look as one who is unhappy. This may be illustrated in many ways.

Paragraphs 13 and 14. Soundness is a matter of being complete, a complete unit. Soundness is without separation. A sound building or bridge is a structure that is made up of many units all bound together in a single unit. You would not think of a building made of many parts all separated as being a sound building. Soundness and wholeness are synonymous. The sound voice in this instance like the "sound" mind in a previous lesson refers to the Unified consciousness in action. No man is sound when he thinks of himself as a departmental being nor is his mind sound when it functions partially nor does he speak soundly when he voices but half the Truth. Truth is that which is true of God for God is all and God is One.

Paragraph 15. Wherever one group or race or nation segregate themselves as a chosen people, a distinct people, in some sense more directly related to or favored of God, they are not a sound people and their doctrines are never sound. God is no respecter of persons and His creation is all manifestation and they are all included impartially within himself. It cannot be that some people are not the chosen of God and others are the chosen of God. He created all men and therefore all people are the chosen of God. All people are God in manifestation just as all forms of plant life are the manifestations of nature. Equality is in the fact and outward equality is dependent upon the degree to which we have embodied through realization the universal Fact.

Paragraphs 16, 17, 18 and 19. Progress is made,

not through denial, but through the practice of habitually unifying all things with the Source. Unified with the Source, all things begin to manifest their likeness to the source and all appearance to the contrary disappears like ignorance in the presence of knowledge or shadows in the presence of light. To deal with fact is to dispel fancy. To work with fancy is to work with nothing and to accomplish nothing. To achieve something one must work with something. Something can never be made out of nothing.

Paragraphs 20 and 21. Whether your face is radiant with joy or clouded with sorrow, it is the same face but appears differently under different influences. The flesh is just as much manifest spiritual substance whether diseased or whole. Only the influence back of it needs to be changed. When the consciousness is expanded to its true state of Knowing the allness and oneness of God, the flesh automatically manifests this condition. It then is the return of the flesh to its true state as radiant Substance of the Word of God.

Paragraphs 22 and 23. The Kingdom of reality is all about us and the only trasition we need to make is to discard our notion that it is a remote place. All that God is is within, through, and around all men and man himself is included in that allness of God. There is nothing he can do about it but accept it and, in accepting it, living in harmony with it, he becomes aware of it.

Paragraphs 24 and 25. Cause and effect are one and to know the truth is to be instantly free. To know God as health is to be instantly well. To know God as supply is to be instantly supplied for the one presupposes or includes the other. There can be no separation.

Paragraph 26. We must come to the realization

that we are on the way back to the Father's house and not moving out away from it. We are progressing toward unity and not diversity. "Behold our God is One" is the song of the returning soul.

Paragraph 27. The close of the lesson should be self-explanatory but may be illustrated and enlarged upon as the leader is inclined or inspired. The whole point of the entire lesson is to get away from the formed opinions of man which have led him into the sense of separation and to bring him into the consciousness of his Oneness with the Universal whole, his likeness to the whole, and his access to all that there is in Infinite Space.

CHAPTER VIII

MAN

1. As in the preceding lesson it was impossible to study the nature of God without including man, so in this lesson it will be impossible to consider man without a further study of God. The one presupposes the other and they are inseparable. It is impossible to have a king without a kingdom and it is impossible to have a kingdom without a king. It is inconceivable to imagine a creator without his creation and certainly there could be no creation without a creator. They are but the two aspects of a single thing and without the one there could not be the other. Man is therefore an indispensable part of the Universal whole.

2. The Masters' thought of man is that he is in his true estate, always active, and is that through which Principle works or comes into manifestation. As they often put it: "Man projecting God; Man becoming God; the very Ideal of all Perfection; God selective but completely universal." Selection evidently came about through man's thought entirely. The Masters' thought is always that man must make the selection but in that he can never carry that selection out of the Whole or out of complete Principle or Spirit. And that means, of course, that man never does get away from his true Being or true origin. Every man is his own determining factor and that factor is always absolutely one with Principle, never separated and never dependent upon anything but Principle.

3. Man as man can never be a completely independent organism for he is inseparably united with

the whole. How could he remove himself out of infinity? He only imagines his isolation and that imagination is the sole source of his limitation. It is purely imaginary. The extent of his free will, or right of selection, cannot be carried beyond his imagination for, in fact, he is always united in and with his source. He only needs to rid himself of his vain imaginings and accept the inevitable and he is at once in his rightful place with the Universal system. He is king only in the sense that he has the privilege of carrying out the laws of the Kingdom and any king who disregards the laws of his kingdom does not remain king for long. Kingship is subject to the laws of the kingdom just as are the subjects and they are all units in a single system with the law superseding at all times. Only through the binding influences of the law does the kingdom remain an harmonious unit.

4. Man is triune but that trinity is never separated; it is always one. You understand all the attributes of man if you understand Man. The Greeks knew this and expressed it in their statement: "Man, know thyself." It is very evident that we have not begun to know ourselves, our importance, our Divinity; Divinity meaning, of course, that Man is a part of the whole and, as such, does know all and IS the All in manifestation.

5. There can be no triangle unless the three lines which form its sides are joined together in unity. Unless they are joined, there are only three lines and not a trinity at all. The trinity is dependent upon unity and their unity is the trinity. Man's business is not to dissect himself until he understands his trinity which would only be diversity. Man is progressing back to his Father's house and his progress in this direction is to discover himself as a unit, the

undifferentiated position which he occupies in the Universal scheme.

6. It is always possible for man to improve his consciousness to the point where he becomes God-like. That was the first thought in the Divine Right of Kings. It was not for the king to put himself up as the only Divine Ruler. All mankind should be Divine Rulers and rule as Kings but always with that expression of Love which is Service. Man stands One with his own Divinity and he is then of Service always. He never exalts himself above another. If he is an egotist, he destroys himself. He cannot be an egotist for long. Man's kingship arises from his sense of oneness with the whole and egotism arises from the sense that he is a separate ego within and of himself. Therefore, egotism is the greatest violation of the natural law of his being and produces the most disastrous results.

7. The translation of the Bible is in error where it says that man was created in the image of God. The "in" should be left out so that it reads, "Man IS the image of God." The word "in" does not appear in the original. And right here we find illustrated the major trouble with the orthodox conception. They all try to make God in the image of man and, in taking this attitude, they have created something that man cannot understand. Man can understand himself and, if he thinks of God as another personality like himself, only in larger proportions, he can never understand the true relationship that exists between himself and his source. But, if he understands that he is the universal individualized or that he is as an individual what God is universally, he has something which he can comprehend. If we leave out the "in," then man is the image of God. "I am God" is the great statement. It belongs to

man wholly. The image or likeness means the *exactness* in the old Sanskrit. The name and nature of cause and effect are always interchangeable for the one is essentially the counterpart of the other. The activity of cause is the life and form of the effect.

8. Some people quite naturally ask that, if this be true, why did Jesus always say that "I am the son of God," but never "I am God?" But this is only one of His statements. He said, "I and my Father are one." Then the translators, failing to understand the next sentence: "You are God as you present God, therefore I present God to you," left that completely out. Yet he said, "He that hath seen me hath seen the Father—God."

9. It should be remembered also that the name "I am God" was the unspeakable name to the Ancients. The theory was that it was never to be made as an audible statement. Its utterances were in the silence of their own souls and the only way it was ever to be voiced was in the natural radiation of authority, perfection, and power that emanated from this inner secret acknowledgment. "The Father who seeth in secret shall reward thee openly" is the thought. It is the Silent name of the Silent being of God, the inner and universal fact of all creation. In a previous talk we noted that another meaning to the statement, "I am God," is, "I am Silent." The "I am God" is the silent witness within the nature of man to a Universal fact. It is the name hidden within the name Jesus Christ and the secret name of every man that hath breath, and that name is the Breath.

10. It was considered blasphemous to make this audible statement and the people of Christ's time construed His statements as inferring that the unutterable NAME was applied to Himself. They condemned Him by their own inference regarding His

112

statements. But He was true to the law of the mystics and, though many of His statements inferred the fact, He did not utter it. "Thou hast said," "I am," "He that hath seen me hath seen the Father," all infer this same fact but, whatever He may have said in His heart, He is never credited with voicing the fact outwardly that, "I am God." The theory is that man IS the word himself and his own presence in the Universe is the spoken evidence and needs no further utterance. In the beginning was the Word — the word became flesh and when man appears in creation he IS that word unspeakable in sounds or syllables for he is the completed word as he stands. If I AM anything, the living embodiment of it, it is self-apparent and needs no further projection. Everything spoken from this consciousness is the authority of the Universe speaking with all power in heaven and in earth.

11. This was included in his statement that, "before Abraham was, I am," for man, as the formed aspect of God universal, always was and always will be God in evidence. He referred right back to the old Sanskrit law of Abraham: A-Brahm — light — a God. Then came David the Light-bearer, and one who bore the Light to all mankind, and Mary, the Preceptor of Creative Principle. You can bring it all down to the Ah Brahm, which means a Christ Child, the Union of all forces to present the Christ Ideal — man is God — to the world.

12. There should be no distinction made between Universal Man and individual man. No more can such a distinction be made than you can make a distinction between the circumference and the center of a sphere. There is where most of the trouble has arisen. You cannot divide man. Man is One, One with God. "I and my Father are one," was Jesus' true statement and He carried it still further

when He said: "When you pray, pray to the Christ of God; include yourself as the Christ."

13. The Masters do not talk of God *and* man. They are always one in their consideration. There is no separation whatever. There is no priest and a separate congregation. It is the congregation and the priest — all one.

14. Huxley and Darwin and their kind brought forth much evidence regarding mortal man and tried to establish his human or animal origin, hoping thereby to overthrow the creation theory. The Master's attitude is that of the Divinity of man; that he is of Divine origin, never separated from his Divinity in any way. Darwin and Huxley and the others built up their evidence so that there was no Head whatever and that is the reason for their failure. They failed completely to carry it through to Principle. The very last statement of Darwin was: "Beyond this which we have built up still remains Principle, which is a mystery to us." There is no effect without a cause and it is impossible to understand the effect without consideration of the cause.

15. That is why Emil says, "You can do these things just as easily as I do them," with true childlike simplicity. That was the reason for Jesus' great accomplishments, leaving out all egotism. "These and greater things shall ye do."

16. Man as a separate identity can do nothing. "I of myself can do nothing," said Jesus. In his isolated sense man is like a street car with the trolly off the wire. He has lost contact with all motivating power, which is the great underlying cause of all manifestation. The activity, which is cause, not only is the motivating power which produces but also is the effect itself and the only way man can keep going is to keep contact with that which projected him in the first place. "It is the Father within me, He doeth the

works." Cause must always be the motivating force within the effect, for the effect could not propel itself.

17. On this trip to date we have seen many races very different in appearance and custom from each other. The Masters see it all in the light of one consciousness. If we think of them as differing phases of consciousness we are apt to establish for ourselves a separation from that One. The only difference is in the outer for all are motivated by the same inner ideal, which is the Christ, or the I AM God of each one. We must evaluate all men from this point if we would escape the differences that appear outwardly. When this inner becomes the without then there can be no outward difference, hence no strife, no greed, no war. There are many seeds and bulbs but when each has fulfilled itself in outward form it is all one harmonious Nature.

18. It is from this point of view that the Masters look upon reincarnation. They say it is not necessary. It is a human hypothesis only. They say that if there is a light placed in the center of the room the best way to reach that light is to go straight to it. Why circle around it time after time? If you go directly to that light and pick it up and incorporate it, you are through with all reincarnation and karma completely. It is only man's failure to go direct to the central point or fact of life that keeps him in the "wheel of incessant grind." If he will accept that central fact, which is the light that lighteth every man that cometh into the world, he will have arrived and all his going round and round will have ceased, it will have come to an end.

19. All of these great problems that afflict the minds of man are completely overcome when he lives the life of the Masters or the life of his own mastery, the true inner Self. Jesus' firm statement

was that the Truth makes you free. Man gets rid of the idea that he is not God by refusing to accept the negative statements. The statement, "I am God," held habitually as the secret fact within his own nature, frees him from the negative statement that he is not God. It is always better to state the Truth than the untruth.

20. Even your ability to analyze the "I AM" is a direct spiritual evidence of Divinity. If it were not there to analyze you could not analyze it, nor would it occur to you to even attempt an analysis. It is only necessary to accept that Divinity with no negative thoughts or statements regarding it, to be One with it. Analysis, and all efforts to confine it to formalities, keep you from it. Even in mechanics we produce a thing and then account for it afterwards. All attempts to analyze it first only indicate its impossibility. This is true of every progressive step even in our material advancement. How much more should this same procedure apply with things entirely beyond our present system of human reason. The airplane was never accepted as a possibility by the world until it actually flew. A first analysis said it could not fly. Now we have an infinite amount of explanation as to how and why it is so. Facts must always come first and they may be accounted for later.

21. If one is overly cautious and is not fully awake to himself, this may seem like laying hold of your Divinity by means of blind faith but that is not necessary. But, if you take it wholly on blind faith, you have made a separation again and would never get to the goal. It is far better to say "I can" and then go right on to "I AM." "I can" is the potential fact, but "I am" is its fulfillment in your consciousness. Jesus said, "I am the way, the truth and the life." You can never be that which you are not nor

116

can you be anything but what you ARE. If you can become anything, as you put it, you ARE that. It is really not a matter of becoming, it is a matter of Being. Because you accept the "I can't" attitude in any condition or circumstance, you have accepted a division. Jesus said you could not compromise with sin, you cannot deviate from the fact and express that fact.

22. When Jesus considered the suggestion that He turn the stones into bread He realized that the stones were already in existence and in manifestation and He did not need to change the stones into bread as He could stretch forth His hand and the bread was there. "What ought to be IS," is the teaching of the Masters. If He needed bread, He did not need to concern Himself with the stones. He knew that if there was a need for bread it was already in existence and all He needed to do was to give thanks for it.

23. It would be impossible for man to need anything if it were not already in existence. Could you need air if there were no such thing in existence? The need indicates the fact and all one needs to do is to let go the sense of need and accept the fact implied in the need that it is already in existence. That which ought to be IS. This is true of what we refer to as the limitation of the physical body. This is an hypnotic influence of the mind wholly. It has no basis in fact at all. Man brought the sense of material into existence and not the body. The "mortal" body is the hypnotic body and, when man wakes from this state of hypnosis, all this experience will be to him just a nightmare. He wakes to dream no more. If he feels the need of a radiant spiritual body, void of limitation and expressing the glorious Light Body that is his perpetual dream, this is the foreshadowing in his consciousness of his fully awak-

ened state. The thought, the need, the desire is the evidence of the fact that such a state already exists for him and his only achievement is in accepting its existence. This IDEAL state IS the true estate of man.

24. This body does not need to be spiritualized. It is already spiritual but man's false beliefs about it have shut his mind to its radiance and limitlessness. Spirit is always Spirit. Man creates the materiality. There is but one body and that body is Spiritual. It is the Temple of the Living God and God is in the Temple; let all the earth rejoice before God. If you call the body material, it is denying God and profaning the Temple. If you call the body or any true condition material, you are denying God. You are worshiping a material condition more than you are worshiping God. That is how you get into hypnosis. The moment that you deny God you are in a hypnotic influence and the moment you see the body as material you are in a hypnotic influence wherein you deny God.

25. The body is an instrument through which to express God. It is the greatest known instrument to express Spirit. It is brought here definitely for you to present God every moment. Not to present materiality, or hypnosis, or psychism; not to present phenomena, but to present Spirit. We are God. We cannot make a separation and, if we refuse completely all separation, we would be out of all material conditions and all psychic phenomena. This is how man comes to know and understand the One Presence and One Power. It is all One, One Power, One Reality. And everything works and operates under that One Power and One Presence according to its own law. It is not adulterated with any other notion but moves as Itself in its own complete field.

26. You cannot make any differentiation be-

tween the individual soul and the Universal Soul or the Over-Soul. That is, you cannot draw apart. As Jesus said: "That is putting asunder God's Principle." There is a generalization under which every human being works but that is an assembly of Universal Units. There is individual identity but you are one in an assembly of Universal units. So is every human being. All are one and the same, operating under the same harmonious conditions. Always in harmony. Not differentiating from harmony but assembling in harmony.

27. A God-man is a genius, Christ standing forth, man expressing God without reserve or restraint. The reason children are often found to express what we call unusual genius is only that they have not yet been hypnotized with the idea of limitation possessed by those about them. If they continue to escape this hypnotic spell they remain geniuses, or the Divine Self, throughout the earth experience. They do not experience the earth, they experience their universality and the Christ-Self always.

28. To be the Master, the Self, is our great work always. The Masters of the East never say anything less than that America contains 130,000,000 Masters. That means that everyone is a Master. That is, of course, true of the whole world. It is worldwide to them. Every individual IS a Master. Even man's limitation is proof to them of his mastership for only a Master could make himself to appear that which he is not.

29. The greatest presentation of Principle is what the world commonly calls the appearance of an Avatar or Savior. The acclamation, "Behold the King," means that man lives closely to Principle, not that a great personage is coming but one who lives closely to Principle. Others acclaim him the

Avatar or genius. He is but one man standing forth in the character that is potentially the Kingship of every man. Only he had the courage and conviction to take himself for what he IS. "The King can do no wrong," for the moment any wrongdoing enters in, the moment a man accepts himself as less than the King, less than his Divinity, he has thereby become less than his own Kingship. The King is the Master, the Genius, expressing himself in his true nature, and therein is his Kingship. He rules himself, for he is in his own Kingdom. The Kingdom of heaven is within. This Kingship which he is is also his message to all men. Not that he is King but that every man is a King within his own kingdom, a master over himself and his own environment, for he lives in reality; he lives as he is and in a realm of things as they really are. This is the Path which He shows to others or the life He lives becomes the path of life for all mankind.

30. His appearance or reappearance upon the earth is not dependent upon any condition of spiritual unfoldment for He is that Thing in its fullness. He steps right through all unfoldment and lives one with Spirit always. The idea of unfoldment belongs to man and his own theories. The Master has only accepted the state in which he was created from the beginning, the Image and likeness of God, the embodied nature of Infinity or Divinity.

31. These illumined souls or Masters or Avatars do not write books because of the utter simplicity of their teachings. There is nothing to be said or written about "I AM," for it is complete within itself. The life they live is its own revelation, it is the book of life revealed, opened as a scroll and needs no testimony but itself. When you reach the top you pull the stairs up with you. Therefore, there is no teaching to give. There is but the fact of life, the

Truth of life revealed as itself, as it always has been and always will be. Steps as man would teach and write about are but degrees to which he lets go of falsity. He had better let it all go at once for, to "think yourself there is to be there," as the Masters say.

FOR THE TEACHER

Paragraphs 1 and 2 bring us back to the eternal Unity of all things and the inseparable relationship which exists between God and man. This point cannot be stressed too strongly for the illumined have always taught that there is not God and Man, there is only God. Man is a unit in and with the Infinite and, as such, contains within himself all the potentialities of Infinity and all of Infinity is accessible to him. Man is ONE in and with the Universe.

Paragraphs 3, 4 and 5. Man cannot be an independent organism in the Universe for his whole being is dependent upon the source from which he came and his mastership is wholly dependent upon taking his place in the Universe. This is the prodigal returning to his Father's house, that point where he dwells and lives in relationship with his source. He can be nothing of himself.

Paragraph 6. The Divine right of Kings, the divinity of man, lies in exercising the power that his position in the Universe presents; not in controlling others but ruling within his own kingdom, himself, under the law that governs all things. "Greater is he that ruleth his own spirit than he that taketh a city." Inward rulership is the Mastery of the Masters. The Master does not prate his mastership. Christ did not attempt to reveal his own divinity but to acquaint all men with their own divinity.

Paragraph 7. Man is the personification of the

Divine Principle or the individuality of the Universe. Man is the personal God or the embodiment of the Universal and Impersonal.

Paragraphs 8, 9 and 10. The "I am God" does not belong to the sense which man has of himself but the projected and ideal man of the Oversoul. For this reason the wise never have proclaimed to the world that "I am God." They knew it within themselves, acknowledged it before God, but before the world they became the expressed fact and let it stand for itself. This is the ark of the covenant, the silent acceptance of the secret relationship which exists between creator and created.

Paragraphs 11, 12 and 13. Brahm was one name for God and a Brahm means a God. Before I was God individual, I was God Universal, for the one is dependent upon the other. They are one and the same thing, always have been so and always will be so. "I am with you always."

Paragraph 14. There can be no material accounting for man, for matter does not produce intelligence, nor intelligence attain to spirit. Spirit is cause and, as cause, it endows its creation with the power of thought and being or expression. There is no determination for anything except as the expression of Spirit or cause.

Paragraphs 15 and 16. The habit of attributing certain powers to others and denying them for oneself is the practice that forever keeps man from arrival at his own mastery. The thought should always be that "if he has achieved I also may achieve, for what is potential with one is potential within all. Man's arrival at the height of achievement is only the revelation of myself." He has attained or manifested that which I AM should always be the thought.

Paragraph 17. To see all men as the embodiment

of the same potential character, to see all men as the Christ, is to instantly dissolve all differences for things equal to the same thing are always equal to each other. This is the secret of the new order of things where peace and goodwill will be established in the earth. Only in the sense of difference can greed and strife develop.

Paragraphs 18 and 19. Can we not see once and for all that this running to and fro in the earth is entirely beside the pont and that it is all due to the fact that we avoid the main issue? To accept the central fact of life is to become entirely free from all those ideas and processes which are less than the fact. If one arrives, he is free from the processes of arriving, and man must learn to begin his life at the beginning, which is God.

Paragraph 20. "What man can conceive he can achieve," is an old adage but it has a meaning even above that for what he can conceive, he IS. It is as impossible to conceive a thing that is not already a fact as it would be to breathe if there were no air. The function within the nature of man is indication of that fact with which the function deals. It would be impossible for the cry to originate in the nature of man if there were not already the supply, the completed fact in the nature of God. And the fact precedes the desire in man for the desire is the recognition of the fact and its existence.

Paragraph 21. Caution is the retardant; boldness is not presumptuous when dealing with facts. It is merely accepting that which has already been proved in the lives of others as equally true of yourself.

Paragraph 22. It is not necessary to convert one form into another for the other is already there just as truly. It is training the mind to know this, to work in the realm of reality, and not always to be trying to make something over into another form of reality. Two plus two equals four and three plus three equals six and it is not necessary to try to make one over into the other. They are both manifest facts already.

Paragraph 23. A continuation of the same truth.

Paragraph 24. You are not making your body over or changing your world, you are only recognizing reality and discarding all false notions about everything.

Paragraph 25. The body is already the temple of the living God. It needs to be freed of the money changers, dealers in comparative values, the ideas of individual profit. The Lord of Hosts and King of Kings must be admitted into the consciousness so it may express through the body what IT IS.

Paragraph 26 is obvious.

Paragraph 27. The Master, the Genius, the God man are all one and the same thing and this is but man being MAN, being Himself, void of the opinions of race experience.

Paragraph 28. There is no work for man but being the Self for when the Self appears he enters the realm of completion. He is forever busy, however, for he has only then begun to work.

Paragraph 29. The Divine self of each man is the Avatar, the Savior of his own being, but he must accept his Savior, be that SELF.

Paragraph 30 is a continuation of Paragraph 29.

Paragraph 31. Man arriving at his divine estate is the book of life opened before all men as a scroll, the seals of the book are broken and man as he is appears.

CHAPTER IX

LIFE

1. The "Life of the Masters" is Life the way they live it. They live life as it is. Their attitude toward life is that it is the action of the One Principle, never divided or separated from its source. They live life true to that Principle and thus, they show the way for all to live true to that Principle of Life. To them life is not a theory of existence, it is an actual fact, a fact with no beginning and no ending. The individual must come to this one attitude of living which comes through the one attitude of thought toward it. They say that it is God expressing through the human individual, the highest and most select channel through which life manifests. Thus life can manifest in a more select activity or complete form through the human individual.

2. They see the One Life emanating in and through all things. In fact, everything that has being is of the very essence of this one life. The human being only postulates life as beginning when this form came into existence through which life could manifest, when in reality life existed prior to the form and even produced the form. That was only the beginning of form and not the beginning of life. Life has always existed and it will always exist. If we select life, or measure it in some specific manner, we may manifest it in that select form. It, of itself, flows freely and universally without cessation or limitation. Consequently, we may select and use that life force, as we would say, in a degenerate way where we do not allow it to manifest in its greatest degree or potency. The human being can

use it in that way but it is only the fault of the individual or the group and is not in any way the fault of life itself. Life, if we will allow it to be so, is the all-knowing, all-seeing and all-being activity of Principle. If we allow it to flow through us in its highest attributes, we cannot help but live by expressing these very conditions which are in its nature.

3. When we accept life as it is, the body becomes a living, breathing unit, expressing life to its fullest degree. The reason that it does not express to its fullest degree is because of the limitation which the human unit puts upon life. We turn it in many ways whereas, in reality there is but one way and that is life in its fullest expression.

4. The Hindoo thought of the three score and ten years of man's allotted time is that this should be the time of man's greatest accomplishment. At seventy, man should reach his majority or his greatest realization of life. Then, they say that man should live five times as long as it takes him to reach his majority. The Western world has completely missed this meaning.

5. Man should not be limited even to that space of time. They do not limit man at all. If you accomplish three score years and ten, you should accomplish all life and all conditions of life. That is not putting a limitation upon it. Five times is not a limit because you can make it five thousand times if you wish. Man does, usually, after he has reached seventy, begin to think more along Spiritual lines. This tendency begins to develop after forty.

6. When Jesus said," In the midst of life ye are in death," he was not warning the people that they are always face to face with death. He expressed astonishment at the condition of death among men when they lived in the midst of life continually. Man only

126

needs to live life as it is, accept it as it is, and not measure it by years and material standards. You are eternal life right here and now if you would only recognize it. But life is not something that is to come; it is here at this very moment in which you live. People separate themselves from the life which IS by trying to live in the past or the future. But the past is dead and the future is only born in the eternal now. All the life of Infinite Space moves at this very moment and whosoever will may drink of that life freely. You do not even need to try to live eternally for, if you are alive at all, you are in eternal life and all you need to do is to so live it. Forget the past, do not try to project yourself into the future for NOW is the only acceptable time. You are in eternity NOW.

7. It is held as a theory that the masters often receive their enlightenment in the springtime of their thirty-seventh year. But there is no limitation except that put on it by the individual. Thirty-seven in the Sanskrit means Eternity because you can repeat the thirty-seven or the seven as many times as you wish, since it completes the octave. It does not necessarily refer to years at all but to the extension of the individual consciousness into the Life Universal or into its true spiritual expression.

8. Instead of the awakening which comes to man being a matter of years, it simply means that he becomes mature in himself and many of the ideas given him by the race are nullified in this maturity of soul. False ideas are crowded out of consciousness as the swelling bud pushes back the leaves that enfold it and then the inner character stands forth. It is not intended as a second childhood when the old man becomes childish but he becomes the child capable of entering the Kingdom. He loses the sense of importance in respect to the material world and

127

its many problems and begins to live in the realization of life as it is unfolding in him.

9. Our scientists are telling us that there is not a human body in existence over seven years old. That is, the cells are completely renewed every seven years. That is not putting a limitation on life, because life moves in cycles and not years and you cannot limit a cycle. It has no real beginning and it does not come to an end. It is the eternal process of fulfilling itself and the eternal renewing process going on within the instrument through which it expresses. Life does not end at seven nor does life ever end. Life is eternal. There is not a thing in existence that does not have life. All planets are alive. Everything has life. The rock has life.

10. When we express life in its true and unlimited natural expression, we can and will be our own books and teachers. Also, if you can appreciate the fact that all of the cells of the body are renewed every seven years, you will begin to realize the possibilities of life. If you will keep your mind continually renewed as the processes of life unfold, you will begin to see that life might just as well go on cycle after cycle, or continuously. The buds on a tree are just as young whether that tree be old or young. And the bud has the completed tree within itself. That tree does not grow old except through the limitation of years that man puts upon it. Nothing grows old except through the concept that man places upon it. The Scriptures teach that he was given dominion over all things. Life can not be measured by years and we should cease to attempt it. Life can be measured only by itself and life is eternal, everpresent, and limitless. It is the vital action of the entire system called the Universe or God. Man places the limitation on time by delineating time for his own convenience and that delinea-

tion does not restrict life or time by any means, except so far as his manifest possibilities are concerned.

11. This is, in all probability, the only plane and the only condition where death is recognized. Christ said: "Let the dead bury their dead." The true man places no limitation on time. The mortal man alone does this. We get into the mortal or physical only by the placement of time or the designation of time for man's convenience. We have gone on and built up a great world of supposition, a great barrier of supposition between ourselves and the true condition. We have been led to see that barrier as insurmountable. Consequently, many of our philosophers have said that life is unknowable and could not be solved. Of course it cannot be solved when you put up barriers against it.

12. The life of the masters is not passed in what the world would call gainful occupations. They have passed that. Their life is of Service always, many of them going about from place to place assisting in what we would look upon as material ways, with material things. We have never seen them accepting anything from anyone for themselves. We have seen them give out food and clothing and supplies of all descriptions. A Master is a servant. If he is a Master, he is above the world and the world can give him nothing. He must reverse the process and he in turn gives to the world.

13. In this service they do not seem to seek out people nor do people necessarily seek them out. The Masters come across those in need in their everyday life as they go about among the people. They also assist in a universal attitude as well through thought and the projection of thought. They also project conditions of perfection into the whole world. Of course, where an individual does appeal to them for

help there is always the assistance ready. We have seen them not only assisting the individual but great groups of individuals. But, even while they are going on with that work, they are evidently sending out emanations to the whole world which in time will cure the condition they are working on locally. They say it is necessary to work locally to assist people to a better understanding and, in many cases, a better understanding comes through the furnishing of food and clothing or a better condition in which to live.

14. The Masters do go out among the people and the people do appeal to them for help very often and the condition which they are under is corrected almost immediately. The help given is only to show a better way to accomplish than that which they are using at the time. They do not go out and preach and proselyte at all. They walk among the people and the people who recognize them may ask for assistance in any way they wish—for healing, food, raiment, or shelter and they receive it. But they are shown that they, themselves, do it and not the Masters. It is not what the Masters have that they receive but the people themselves have built up that which is brought to them through their own attitude of thought; not what someone else has but what they have and what belongs to them. It does not necessarily follow, however, that you must appeal in order to get assistance.

15. The statement that the servant is worthy of his hire does not mean that one may commercialize healing. That means that the individual who thus serves is worthy of a higher life, worthy to become a Master and not a servant. Of course the Master is the greatest servant, for his entire life is spent in service, for that is the field in which he works and expresses his mastership.

16. In the matter of food, the Masters consume far less than we do. We have known them to eat no more than three grains of rice a day but they take in enough pranic substance to support their bodies for long periods if necessary. They masticate their food thoroughly. They can chew these three grains of rice all day and, by the time they have finished, they have taken enough prana to last their bodies at least twenty-four hours. They have no set time for eating for they do not work with time as men measure it. They eat whenever they feel like it. We have never known them to recognize meal hours as we recognize them. They can go without food completely for hundreds of days.

17. As far as we know they take very little sleep, not in excess of two hours a day, and they are conscious during these two hours. It is a well known fact that you can get along without sleep, if you know how to live without wasting your energies or contracting your consciousness through separating yourself from the Universal energies. The Western world and the way they live causes sleep to become more or less a condition brought about by, as we say it, a toxic state of the body. The toxic condition overcomes to a great extent the rebuilding process of the body and thousands of people are in that toxic state instead of being in a true condition of sleep. When Jesus said, "Awake thou that sleepest," he meant to arise from that comatose condition and then you are out of the influence to which you have become subject.

18. The Western world consumes at least ten times as much food as the body needs and then consumes energy to digest that food. That energy which is used to handle this nine-tenths of the surplus food that we take unnecessarily could be used much more effectively to build up the body. It is a well

known fact that today the Western world eats at least ten times as much food as is healthful. If we would take life direct or energy direct from the ethers, we would be adding energy to our bodies all of the time instead of giving it out to assimilate food. It would go directly to every organ of the body and rebuild and renew it.

19. It is not necessary that one be with a Master or contact a Master in any sense to understand life and its possibilities. Life is perfectly understandable at every corner of the earth. It is Omnipresent and anyone may contact it if he will turn his attention in that direction and get away from the mere forms which life uses and through which life expresses.

20. If you will take the simple attitude that all the life that you can live is LIFE and begin to exalt life, you will then be doing what you would do if you were living with them. There is nothing phenomenal regarding their life at all. Usually people going to them look only for phenomena. If we live life, we cannot help but understand life. Life is a process of inward force working itself out into outward form. It is the vital principle of the Universe animating all space and all form.

21. So many people have the notion that the Masters lay down certain rules for your daily practice, a certain daily regime of mental and physical exercises, but this is not so. There are many who lead out with this sort of teaching, of course, to the point where the student recognizes that he himself is a Master. Then the way is opened to meet the actual Master. The moment that man gets into his mind that there is any life to live other than the One life, he is out of harmony completely. The difficulty is with his mental application always. Man did not fall and die spiritually, he simply got himself out of harmony with life and this resulted in all his diffi-

culty. The moment life becomes hard, it is not life. That individual is out of life just to the degree that any inharmony develops and this state should be a warning for him to get back into life as it is.

22. Children are happy because they live life abundantly. They put no limitations upon life whatever. The moment we put limitation upon life we cease to live abundantly. There is not a limiting condition in life. Life could not limit itself. It could not be kept away except through your own attitude of thought toward it. No two individuals have the same vision of life. It is quite often illustrated in this way:It is said that only children and sages are happy because the child has not developed a material sense of value and the sage knows that the material has no value. To them form is not the point of consideration but living life.

23. One man may look at life through a very narrow opening in a wall. That person says, "I see all of life." The view may face a hill where there is nothing but rocks. The next may see trees; the next one sees animated forms moving about. If we look through but one small opening, we soon hypnotize ourselves into believing that there is no other life within the great expanse of the Universe of life. If we would take this attitude alone: see the Universe as embodying and expressing the One Infinite life, then we would expand our vision to take in all of life and there would be no limitation whatever for us.

24. The Masters never take conscious life. It is not necessary to take conscious life because man can assimilate into his consciousness all of the life elements, bring them into existence in himself, live them, and be always one with them. Consequently it is not necessary to take conscious life at all.

25. Many people ask the question why it is that

the people of India are afraid of the lower forms of life. Not all people in India are masters, even though they have been taught that there is but one life. They do not see all they have been taught any more than Americans see or live all they have been taught.

There are only a few of the lower classes who are bound in this way because they have been taught to worship these conditions. It is thus that they fear them.

26. And why do the Masters not raise the people out of that condition? How could they raise you out of a condition if you would not accept that raising? They cannot inject their own minds into you. They can only show you the path which they have traveled. If you will not see that path you must make your own until you are ready for a better way. All of the higher castes, even the great Maharajas, work for the better condition in India but they cannot do the overcoming for the masses nor transform them into higher beings. That is the work of the individual always.

27. It is a misconception to think that the Masters live an ascetic life. We have never found them so living. You will find them in a loin cloth or in the highest walks of life! You will not find them isolating themselves at all. There are a few, a very few compared to the whole, living in seclusion in order to give out more fully to the whole world certain conditions for betterment. But they are only groups who come together for that specific purpose. They do not live an ascetic life at all.

28. You may see a Yogi living an ascetic life for a certain time for a certain purpose only but then, they never allow asceticism to become hypnotic. Yogi means living for a great experiment. Many of

the so-called "holy men" of India live a complete ascetic life but usually they are beggars and not Masters. A great many of them are as dirty and as filthy as anything you can imagine. They are leeches on humanity and nothing else. But they are not the Masters. Just because a man goes about saying mantrams, or sitting in Samadhi, he is not thereby a Master.

29. We have never known of one of these who has reached a high accomplishment begging of anyone but they are giving all of their time to the betterment of humanity. They do not beg anything to give away even. They have, as they put it, all that they want and to spare always. They do not go around and beg for others to give. They do not organize charitable institutions. They go out and assist all of the time, separating themselves by their accomplishments. There are thousands of people in India who are giving out continually and yet, we have never known any of them to take a penny from anyone. The beggars who call themselves "holy men" are such only by their own designation. They have nothing to do with the Masters.

30. Life is always a matter of giving. To draw on the Universal life that flows freely throughout infinite space is the privilege of anyone and his way of living life should be to receive from this source and then give it out to all who are around him, inspiring them to seek life where he has found it. This is not only the work of the Masters, but it is the work all men should be doing. This is living life as it should be lived and is really the only life there is. To merely receive from those about you is not life at all but a constantly contracting existence. To seek life from the material world is to lose it.

FOR THE TEACHER

Paragraph 1. It should become evident to the mass of humanity that life as revealed by the illumined has always been portrayed in its universal and eternal aspect. That life which is manifest in form is only the outcropping of the vital essence that fills infinite space. Life is not confined to a period of expression through form but is and forever remains the movement of the creative force that produced form in the first place and that form was produced for the sole purpose of affording it expression. No one lives truly until he knows that life is moving in and through him and eternally seeking a fuller, freer, richer expression always.

Paragraphs 2 and 3. Life being universal, it is universally expressed in every form, and when the sense of separateness disappears from the mind of man he may enter more fully into its activity and align himself more completely with its purpose. Only in the human consciousness do complications seem to develop and life and consciousness are so inseparably united that before man can realize life in its fullness he must expand his consciousness to see and live life as it is. Only his mental reactions to the appearance keep him from this fuller life.

Paragraphs 4, 5, 6, 7 and 8. The text of these paragraphs shows clearly that it is the period during life when man's outward thought, his thought developed through his material contacts, so greatly interferes not only with his life but with his capabilities generally. It is this period of false estimates of life, his world, and himself that impedes his entire existence and it is only prior to this state and occasionally following it that man seems to enter into the real joy of living. The genius is one who seems to a degree to escape this period of thought oppression;

136

one who has the courage or fortitude to go his own appointed course and not let the world thought of limitation hinder him. The reason man, in his later years, seems to live a more spiritual life is that the false run down like an eight-day clock and then his true nature asserts itself. Had this consciousness been preserved through the years of oppression, his body would not have been sapped of its vital forces and his greatest years of usefulness would have been extended indefinitely.

Paragraph 9. The age of the body is not designated by the span of years which we call life. The body is forever renewing itself and the cells and tissues which form the body are constantly being replaced through a perfectly natural process. It is the pattern under which this building process is forced to operate that gives the body its condition of age. We should be continually renewing our minds in accordance with the truth of life and then the pattern for the renewing processes of the body would be such that a more perfect and vital body would be the result.

Paragraph 10. Man is the book of life, the law of God. The governing principle of life is written in his inward parts, and this period of existence should be a process of self-discovery and self-expression. In the unfoldment of man's own nature he learns the secrets of his own being. Study yourself at first hand, the deepest longings of your own inner nature, watch them unfold and you will understand.

Paragraph 11. Sin, according to the Scriptures, is the cause of death. Sin is every thought and feeling that is out of harmony with the purposes of life. These thoughts and feelings make up the opposition to life as it would express itself through the flesh. To remove the obstruction would be the remedy, of course. Instead of perpetuating a consciousness that deprives the body of its sustaining power, thereby separating the body from consciousness in death, one should die to the false consciousness. "Forgetting the things which are behind, pressing forward."

Paragraphs 12, 13, 14 and 15. Life is a matter of progress and not profit as we construe it. Profit is contingent upon our progress and our progress is determined by the kind and quality of our expression. Expression should not be the constant projection of our own limited opinions but living true to the deepest impulses are always true. Only when we descend to the plane of what we call necessity or expediency do we begin to violate our inward sense of what is right.

Paragraphs 16, 17 and 18. "Man shall not live by bread alone." Only enough food is required to supply material for the natural reconstruction of man's body. What is more than this is but giving the functions of the body an excess of labor. One should feed more and more upon the substance that moves in the creative principle of his being and then he would find real nourishment. As food is supplying material for body building, sleep is consuming energies that have been wasted during our periods of false living.

Paragraphs 19, 20, 21. We must learn to contact our good at its source. What we are seeking does not come from another and it will do no good to contact Master or teacher unless we thereby are inspired to seek that in ourselves which he represents to us. "Not everyone that saith unto me Lord, Lord, shall enter in, but He that doeth the will of my Father."

Paragraph 22. The values of life are to be found in the Soul, the Real Self, the inner Master, and not in the world. The world has only the value imparted to it by the awakening of true consciousness.

Paragraphs 23, 24 and 25. Seek to find life as it is in its great universal movements which are revealed in your nature through your own highest ideals and deepest longings. Only when we measure life in our own limited ideas does it become limited in its manifestation through us. Depend upon the Life Universal for supply.

Paragraph 26. Man's individual right to expression cannot be violated in the true processes of life. It is by our own effort that we rise and not by the efforts of others. Vicarious living without effort upon our part is destructive to our own character and well-being.

Paragraphs 27 to 30. Life is action, self-expression, giving. It is as necessary to give in order to live as it is necessary to exhale in the processes of breathing. One should receive from his source and then give of that source in his highest expressions. One first receives from any principle by taking it into his consciousness and then he expresses it in outward performance. This is equally true in the processes of life. To receive without giving or to give without receiving is to make life static through surfeit or exhaustion. To receive from your source and express what you have received in manifesting your greater capabilities is the way of life.

CHAPTER X

THE UNIVERSE

1. The Universe is the sum total of all things visible and invisible that fill infinite space. The Universe is the great whole, composed of all its parts. It might be said that the Universe is another name for God for He identified himself as "I am that I am and beside me there is no other." It is the sum of all life, all substance, all intelligence, all power. In it is contained all knowledge for it is Omniscience. It is the sum of all power for it is Omnipotence. It is the sum of all substance for out of it are all visible things formed. It is all Love for it is bound together in a single system and operates as a single unit. Love is the integrity principle or the binding principle which maintains the universe as a unity and keeps all its operations moving in perfect harmony and regularity.

2. The Masters think of the Universe as the univerality of all things, with every condition and circumstance a portion of that Universe or universality. A person may become separate or he may separate himself in thought from that Universe. Then he becomes a unit which in thought only is separate or apart. But instead of being apart he is still a part of the Great Universe. One may become so separated in thought from that Great Universality that he surrounds himself with apartness or the sense of limitation. He may withdraw so far from that Universality in thought that he falls or descends in his capacities and, thus, he is in a measure separated from that Universality in which he really belongs.

3. Of course it is impossible to separate oneself

or completely exclude oneself from that Universality, for that would be to reduce himself completely to a state of non-existence. But, when he returns to that Universality of Principle in consciousness, he is one with it and is lifted up into a higher state of capability. That is illustrated in the parable of the Prodigal Son. He wandered in many lands and spent his substance but there was a welcome in the Father's house upon his return. Even the brother who had stayed at home was jealous of the reception. But the Father knew that the reception was always there. It is an allegorical picture of how one can extensively separate himself from Universality by thought and recognize that he is feeding on the husks and yet when he decides to return to the Father's house there is everything there for him. In fact, the Father was not even conscious of the separation. It did not matter how far away the son had wandered.

4. All sense of apartness, isolation, limitation is only fictitious for it is impossible for separation to be an actual fact. If it were possible the Universe could not be a whole. David illustrated this fact in his realization that it was impossible to get out of the Universal System when he said: "Whither shall I flee from thy Spirit," and whether he went to the uttermost bounds of the earth, ascended into heaven, or made his bed in hell, that same Universal relationship awaited him. You cannot divide the indivisible.

5. It is the same when death occurs. Many feel that there is a separation there, but in reality, there is no such thing. We can be just as close to those that we feel have departed as we were in what we think of as this life. It is only the separation in our conscious thought. In what we call the Superconscious there is no separation whatever. If we would

let go of that thought of separation there would be no evidence of separation for it exists only in consciousness. It might be more truly stated that separation exists only in unconsciousness when one is unconscious of the true state of being.

6. Separation is only an appearance for in reality there could be no such thing. If the Universe is a single Unit and all things within it are eternally united into a single system, how and where could any separation exist? In fact, it could be only an imagined state. Ignorance of the facts is the only kind of separation that can exist and illumination would completely eliminate that. Behold our God is One, say the Scriptures, and if God is the great ONE, all things and all people are included within him and, being included within him, they are one in and with him.

7. Our being is a complete Universe in itself and it acts in perfect harmony if we let go of every thought of inharmony or separation. The thought of harmony returns us to the unity of Principle. We can think of ourselves so far out of harmony that sickness and disease and discordant conditions come about but they are only that which is out of harmony. If we would keep in complete Universal harmony in thought there could be no inharmonious condition come into our lives . . . not one . . . because whenever we vibrate in harmonious relation with the Universal Principle no inharmony can manifest. It is perfectly possible for it to be so.

8. We make it possible ourselves for inharmony to manifest by the reduction of the vibration of our bodies and in no other way. We allow what should be the impossible to take place. When we look upon complete accord as an impossibility, we worship discord instead of worshiping harmony. That was the

very teaching that Jesus gave out when He said that you of yourself are always harmonious. He referred directly to that harmony of Principle which in reality we always manifest and which we could not help but manifest if we would let go of that personal, egotistical desire for direct service from our neighbor instead of giving Service always. Our expectancy should be from above and our attitude toward the world as giving.

9. One of the easiest ways to isolate ourselves from harmony is to demand service from another instead of giving of our service all of the time. It does not matter if we direct it to one individual or a million individuals. When demanding service from others we are always in that separation but when in service to all we are completely immersed in universality. When we give of ourselves we come nearer and nearer to that Universality where we belong.

10. It takes no energy from our bodies to give out Service, Love, and Harmony but it does take energy from our bodies to give out inharmony or discordant conditions or to give out negative thoughts or words. All positive words or words of accord add energy to our bodies every instant that we are giving them out. Not only that, but we create an influence that returns and surrounds us with emanating energy.

11. One does not need instructions from a Master nor does he need to learn from a book what is true to the processes of the Universal life in him. One knows when he violates the law of life just as easily as one knows when the principles of music have been violated. Instantly a discord is recognized by anyone, whether he has studied music or not. The moment any discord or unpleasantness arises in the nature of man, that instant he should know that he

is violating the law of his being. It is not only a violation of the law of his being but it produces inharmonious results in his body. All discordant emotional and mental states are sins against man's true nature. Everything that produces an harmonious effect in man's nature, that which gives him a sense of peace, freedom, power, and harmony, is in direct harmony with life and only harmonious results prevail.

12. Man is exactly the same as a test tube in a chemical laboratory. If we add harmonious solutions we get harmonious results. Otherwise we set up an inharmonious condition wherein we get either inharmonious results or no results at all. We might see great turbulence in a test tube but that is not inharmony if the correct chemicals are placed in that test tube. It is the same in our bodies. We never set up inharmony if we induce or give out only harmonious thoughts and feelings. It is absolutely impossible for us to set up inharmony if we give out harmony, because we surround ourselves with an influence that is completely harmonious. And, if it is all harmony, no inharmony can manifest through that influence. It is all controlled through consciousness and we become perfectly conscious of harmony, far more so than we can become conscious of inharmony, because harmony is our natural state. That is done by refusing to project our vision to inharmony.

13. If people think that they cannot properly discriminate in the matter of consciousness, they can give out Love to the best of their ability and refuse to give out anything else but Love. That will bring them accurately to harmonious conclusions. Jesus placed Love before everything else. There is a little book written by Henry Drummond entitled *Love, the Greatest Thing in the World*, which gives

the complete key to the harmonious solution of every condition that comes up. It is the simplest little book ever written and has a wide circulation. It takes only about ten minutes to read it but it takes a lifetime to live it. In the living of it there is perfect harmony and perfect freedom.

14. If one should take a negative stand and deny the Spiritual, that does not change the spiritual at all. It could not change Spirit for Spirit is eternally unchangeable, but your wrong ideas would slow up your own progress. We should not concern ourselves with what the other person does or what we think he should do, because we cannot tell when his actions or creations will bring him into direct harmony again. Jesus said, "Loose him and let him go." He thus gave him the privilege of incorporating the Christ consciousness. He saw everyone as the Christ. That very statement: "I see the Christ in every face, in every form," is indicative of His attitude.

15. Do not let the world tell you what it is like for it cannot do so. It is not what it appears to be. It appears to be limited but it is not, for it is formed out of the Universe and Science tells us that each cell is a replica of the Universe. You must learn to find out what the world is like by knowing what the Universe is like and then you will be able to tell the world what it is. Only in this manner can you be free for you are expressing only what your own consciousness is. Look through the surface until you see the inner reality and you will find that "Nothing in this world is single, All things by a law Divine with one another's being mingled," and there is perfect harmony and perfect freedom for yourself and for the world.

16. "When the first man was born, your Christ was born," is the true Christ message. "Before Abraham was I am," "The glory which I had with

thee in the beginning before the world was." Add love to all statements and they move in harmony with the Christ as He taught. We can so surround one with Love that that very influence floods in upon him and it may in an instant change his whole life, his whole thought. We are not dominating him when we surround him with Love for that is his native environment. We are only placing an influence that he may accept, thus changing the whole course of his life, and we may also change the whole course of our own lives and thoughts. We are but seeing him as he really is, seeing him as God sees him. This does not hinder or influence him but it frees him from hindrance and influence, because we are surrounding him with that influence in which he was created, that state in which all men live in reality.

17. It is far better to love your enemies and pray for them who persecute you because you merely exalt yourself and at the same time help to free them from those characteristics which cause them to act as your enemies. You are doing a double service both to yourself and to them. The gift is to the giver and comes back most to him. Then, too, sometimes our so-called enemies bring our thoughts out into the clear light of day more so than our friends do.

18. Should you have a supposed friend that does you a great wrong, a harm, the consciousness of perfect love can absolutely change the whole aspect of the situation. That is man's privilege, not his duty. And a privilege is the greatest motive for all of our service. It is a real privilege to love your enemies and exalt them because you are thereby exalting yourself. It is the greatest exaltation in the world to exalt your enemy and see him standing higher even than you stand.

19. This practice is the greatest sincerity for to be

sincere is to be without blemish. It is to be whole. The moment that you cut that individual out of your consciousness you have allowed that individual greater privileges than you have allowed yourself. You must exalt him and then you have finished with the matter. If you loose him and let him go before the exaltation, it is not finished, for you still have your own consciousness to mend. It is like this: you never knew that man before he came into your consciousness. Now you are perfectly conscious of him because there was some situation with which you or he needed assistance. The moment you have gained that which was needed and have finished with that person through exaltation, you can loose him and let him go back just as he was before he came into your life. Then, when your duty is finished and the exaltation is complete, you are both free. Both can go your separate ways the same as you did before. Unless this is done the blemish is still in your own consciousness.

20. You see, all imperfection exists in consciousness only. There is to you no imperfection in those whom you have not contacted. The moment you recognize any imperfect state through contact with anyone, that imperfection is thereby brought into consciousness. Before perfect harmony in your nature can be reestablished, that state must be erased and love is the only attitude that will erase it, for love is the Universal Solvent; it restores everything to its native state in the Universal Scheme. Only in this way are you free and only thus can you free the other person.

21. It is impossible to "loose them and let them go" without the element of love. Pity, either for the other person or for yourself, is not the way of release. Pity always binds you closer to the imperfection. You can pity yourself to the extent that you

will tie yourself up with them faster and faster. You can also pity them until you do exactly the same thing. Pity reduces everything to the low estate of the condition involved, while love exalts the same elements into their rightful place in the Universal. Love is the highest thought you can have. Jesus exalted himself and everyone around him through love. Love is the very essence of the Universe and, in perfect love, all things are united into the Universal Whole.

22. To the individual the universe may be large or small, just as his consciousness dictates. It may be a single atom, it may be a complete body, or it may be the one entire Universality of God completely Universal. When we say universal, if we do not limit our thought to any separate division, we are speaking truly. The thought then is all-embracing just as light surrounds and fills all space. There is a very good saying regarding that in the Mahabharata: "When I see Light, I see all universality." That is because Light is the vehicle that carries Universality into complete existence. The moment we exalt a word it becomes light. The Universe is unlimited. There is no limitation outside of the human concept. The animal never limits itself. It is only man that limits himself.

23. The theory of the expanding Universe is not accurate except in that it expands in our thoughts, or rather we expand our conception of the Universe. We are always discovering that it is larger than we imagined. The Universe is constantly expanding and contracting according to your own concept but not within itself, for the Universe is the sum of Infinity. Many people think of the Universe as referring to a single solar system but a solar system is only one cell or atom in a Universe of innumerable solar systems.

24. There is one law governing the Universe for the Universe is One. We need not obey a single law that is less than the One Law. There is but One Law and that is the only thing that we need to obey. A human being does not need to obey even the manifestation of law, which is gravitation. You need not obey even the conscious manifestation of law; you need obey only the law that controls these manifestations. The moment you become unconscious of the manifestation of law you are perfectly conscious of the Law that is All, the Allness or the Universality of Principle. Every manifestation of law then obeys us. We are in complete authority, complete dominion over every manifestation of law.

25. The thought that there are lesser laws, such as the law of matter, brought the idea of materiality or mortality into effect. It was not Adam, it was the man who followed Adam. Matter is but one attitude of consciousness, the same as thought is but one attitude of consciousness. In other words, matter is only a fixed mental habit. Thought and matter are in reality only avenues of expression and neither should be limited in the considerations of men. Adam, of course, did express consciousness but not the mortal consciousness or mortality of consciousness. That was attached to his name long after the advent of Adam.

26. To the Master there is no material universe. The visible Universe to him is the manifestation of Spirit and is, therefore, spiritual in essence and governed by the law of Spirit. It is this knowledge which gives him power and therein is the secret of all individual power. To know the law of Spirit and to live in harmony with that law is always power of unlimited degree. And that law of the Spirit is the law of Love. It is love that governs infinite space and all forms that are projected in space. That is

why the Scriptures say that if you are in love you are in God and God is in you. Love is harmony and therefore keeps all things in harmony not only with itself but with each other. When man is in a consciousness of love or a consciousness of perfect unity with all things, he is in a state of perfect harmony with all things and with all people. Love is, as it might be said, cohesion, or a binding force that keeps all things in relationship to their source. Working in harmony with their source they work in harmony with all projections of that same source. But love will dissolve that which is not in harmony with the Universal order for it demands of everything its complete adherence to the principle of its own nature, which is Spirit. For that reason love destroys hate, greed, selfishness, and self-seeking and the ego that comes from those states of consciousness.

27. Man is a replica of the complete Universe and he is a complete Universe within himself when he includes himself in that Whole. If he would let go of every thought of creed and dogma, he would be completely out of superstition. He would be completely unlimited. The moment that we unlimit ourselves, it can be shown through photographic evidence today that light emanates from every cell of our body. Light, in the same way, emanates from every cell of the Universe. The source of this Light and energy, which invigorates and fills the expanse of the Universe and the Universe of our body, is the Great Central Sun. Cosmic means great; it is the whole of which man is a part.

FOR THE TEACHER

Paragraphs 1 and 2. This lesson, like the ones just preceding, deals with the Universality of all things and shows that all manifest forms are contained within the whole and are an inseparable part of the whole. It also deals with the fact that each individual organism is in miniature what the Universe is in all its infinity. The point in these first two paragraphs is to help the student to the realization that all the immeasurable power and force that moves throughout Infinite space moves also within him and that his attainment in life is determined by the degree to which he becomes conscious of and works in harmony with these forces.

Paragraphs 3 and 4. Man is only isolating himself by ignorance and by perpetuating his own notions of separation. There is nothing in the attitude of God which separates man or relegates him to obscurity and weakness. God is intent always upon fulfilling himself and, instead of moving to exclude man from the blessings that are rightfully his, is seeking always to manifest Himself through man. Man needs but to eliminate his obstructions to the Divine purpose.

Paragraph 5. There is no death! What seems to be death is only that state where man has crowded the Divine Fact of his being so completely out that it cannot longer sustain the body. The life of the body is the Spirit that created it and, when through ignorance the body is completely dominated by false concepts about life, the body has lost all its true sustaining power and, therefore, can no longer function. That is what is called death. The spiritual man, the man that God created and the only man that God knows, lives as eternally as God is eternal.

151

Your ideas live on when the forms through which you have expressed them are destroyed and God's idea of man lives on when it is crowded from the vehicle designed for its expression. They remain one in and with the Father Principle and, whether in the flesh or out of the flesh, all men may be conscious of the eternal Unity that exists if the ignorance which causes the sense of separation is dropped out of consciousness.

Paragraphs 6 and 7. Ignorance is the only enemy of man. Knowledge of the facts brings him into harmony with the forces of infinite space, all of which are friendly and move constructively for his good. In principle there can be no opposition to itself. Therefore, all that there is in the Universe is moving in the very nature of man and his position is the direct point or vehicle in and through which infinite power and possibility is manifest.

Paragraphs 8, 9 and 10. It is impossible for anyone to find peace and harmony so long as they are expecting everything and everybody to do for them what they alone can do for themselves. No one can give us that which we already possess and cannot awaken in us that which we ourselves refuse to express. It is not the world or the people of the world that can give us what we need or serve us in accordance with our need. Every good gift and every perfect gift comes from above. The Law of the Universe moves from Principle, God, through the individual manifestation and then gives of itself, its true nature, to the world in service. If we reverse the process, expect the world and its people to give to us so that we in turn may become happy and harmonious, thereby attaining our Divinity, we can but meet disappointment. God is the beginning and is the Great Servant of mankind. To receive His spirit is to become the Sons of God and then, our attitude toward the world is to bestow our great gifts upon all around us, a gracious and generous service.

Paragraph 11. Man's own nature is the Book of Life and, if he will study the eternal trends of his inner nature, allow the deepest side of his nature to expand and grow, then he will understand himself, the Universe, and the law of the Universe. He will not need any man to instruct him.

Paragraph 12. This should be obvious to anyone who has known turmoil and peace within his own nature. Only when false elements are induced into his nature does this upheaval come and only when he receives into his nature that which is harmonious is he in harmony. Man is the chemist and he mixes within himself that which produces his pains and his pleasures.

Paragraphs 13, 14 and 15. It is as easy for anyone to tell what is in harmony with his nature and the purpose of God moving through him as it is easy to tell the difference between harmony and discord in music. This is as evident to the one who has never studied music as to one who is a finished musician. It is just as easy for the most ignorant to recognize discord and inharmony as it is for a Master to do so. We must learn to discriminate and refuse to let ourselves indulge in any mental or emotional reaction that dulls our sense of perfection.

Paragraph 16. It was not Adam but ignorance that caused man to forget his divinity and it is ignorance that keeps us in bondage when in reality there is no bondage. Infinity fills all time and space and our mission is to awaken to the fact that all of Infinity moves through us and our capacities are measured only by this fact.

Paragraphs 17 to 21. The greatest doctrine of Christ was Love, for love is not only the fulfillment of all law but is the solution for every problem that arises in life. Love is the law of the Universe and, when it becomes the ruling passion of the individual, then he is in harmony with all the forces of infinite space. He that is in Love is in God. Love is first to be developed in the individual as an inseparable Union with the Infinite. Being one with the Infinite you are one with all the manifestations of the Infinite. This does not mean that you are to love the imperfections in the world, in your neighbor, or in yourself. Drop these out of consciousness and make your union with the Divine that is back of this outward mask in which you cannot see or know God.

Paragraphs 22 and 23. Your Universe is the one you see. "The Land thou seest, that will I give unto thee as an inheritance." Back of all things is Light for in the beginning was Light. The light became the life of man. Even our material scientists say that light is the foundation of all manifest form. Therefore, man's real body is not a body of material flesh but a body of light which includes the flesh, for light sustains the flesh in exactly the same sense that oxygen and hydrogen sustain water. When ignorance is withdrawn from consciousness we will see and manifest the light.

Paragraphs 24 and 25. If one obeys the constitution of the United States and gives everyone the right to life, liberty, and the pursuit of happiness, will he not automatically obey every other law in the country? Obedience to the Highest law automatically involves the fulfillment of every obligation to every other law. The law of the Universe is Love and, if one moves in love, conscious union, and oneness with God and man, he will not do any thing that would violate any lesser law. But, in this sense, he would move in an infinitely free and uncircumscribed manner and there would be no sense of bondage by these lesser manifestations of laws.

Paragraphs 26 and 27. The Universe and all that is contained within it is one single system and our mission is to so see it. Not that it matters to the Universe so much, but it makes all the difference to the individual. His release comes in his knowledge of things as they are.

CHAPTER XI

YOUR SELF

1. When Jesus the Christ taught "Unless you become as a little child, you can in no wise enter into the kingdom of Heaven," He gave one of the most profound truths. A child has not yet been hypnotized by the world idea of limitation and lives naturally in harmony with its source. That is why most grown people love to be with children. They radiate the natural harmony of the Universe and that is the natural environment of man. If we would only drop all the ideas that have related us to the world, we would find ourselves in that determination which comes from the Universal movement and we would perform the works that are always seeking to manifest themselves through our nature. "Wherever thou findest self, drop that self," wrote the ancient Hindus and that is still the central teaching of the Masters. Only when habits to the contrary are dropped from the primal nature of man can he hope to live the life which is the only life. Most of our attempts at living are so completely adverse to the purpose and natural trend of life that it only leads to the dissolution of the flesh. "There is a way that seemeth right unto man, but the end thereof is death," said Jesus.

2. Know this: There is nothing that really limits man and keeps him in a state of uncertainty and inefficiency but his own thought. When these thoughts are removed he may enter into the life of the universe with ease and then his life begins to give evidence of its natural possibilities. "In that day when ye think not the son of man cometh," was the

wise instruction of the great Master. All thought that comes into man's consciousness from the world is but a reflex of the impressions so received and man is not a reflector. Man is the projection of the Divine and, only as he allows the deepest impulses of his own nature to express, is he in life as it is.

3. The divine purpose of the law of life is to perfect and refine the nature of man until it is a complete and perfect expression of Itself. When life is lived in this way, without the reserve and restraint caused by the hypnotic spell of induced thought, the nature of man is continually refined. This requires the constant control of the individual until all his nature is a unit in expressing the one single purpose. The determination of this force is then perfect outwardly as it is already a fact in the Universal. Only in this way can man fulfill his destiny and receive the full support of the Universal forces. Many people wonder why God does not manifest through their own ideas and give them what they imagine they want. God no more acts through the ideas of man than the law of nature acts through infertile seeds, except to disintegrate them. God or Spirit is about his own business, fulfilling his own ideal and purpose, and man must come into harmony with this Universal purpose. Then, and only then, will he attain that state of complete childlikeness where he lives life naturally. Natural life is perfect and produces perfect results. Our ideas are either altogether imperfect or incomplete. They have not the nature or purpose of the Universal trend in them, therefore they are only to be discarded and put aside in order that the higher influences may become the determining factors in our entire being.

4. You say you have been taught that the first law of nature is self-preservation and so it is. But

that does not mean that one protects his own life at the expense of another. The law of life moves to preserve and promote life. The life of a Master is one that promotes and preserves life for he lives in harmony with the only life which is. In him there is no revenge and his whole motive is to protect life from every intrusion. That is the secret of Mastery. Until one has mastered that in his own nature which would destroy his life, he is out of life. But when he is free from that which would destroy life he is completely in life. Even Jesus did not condemn those who crucified him but released them from the karma of their own ignorance through the law of forgiveness.

5. The fact is, to hold another in blame or to attempt to place blame upon another, is only to involve yourself in that ignorance. Protect life wherever it is manifest. Guard your own life and the lives of others from all ignorant intrusion. Protect yourself and others from any thought or act which would involve them in anything but the fuller and more harmonious expression of life. To do otherwise is suicidal. Constantly refine your own life by protecting the life all around you. But, to protect others is not only to protect them from bodily violence but to protect them from their own ignorance and the ignorance of others. Free yourself and others from the hypnotism of human thought and see yourself and them as free sons of the highest. Only in this way can you enter into life and to enter into life is to become the master yourself. If someone does you an injury, free him instantly in your own mind and free him from the possibility of criticism or condemnation from others. Always hold him freely in the Universal life.

6. Many people never stop to think why artists paint a halo of light around the saints and masters.

It is because they are illumined and illumination is always there when the veil of ignorance, the cloud of hypnotism, is removed. You even see in some degree this same light around children and it is the emanation of this light that makes you feel peaceful and calm when in the presence of very small children. They are perfectly free vehicles of the Universal life. This is the influence one feels and the light one sees around a Master. He has become as a little child; he is freed from all world ideas that dim the light. Light is life and when one is completely in life he is in light—he IS that light. One who is completely in light lifts everyone into that same light to the degree that they are willing to let themselves respond to its influence. It is nothing supernatural that people should see light emanating from a Master. It is perfectly natural for that is life in its natural state. You have all potentialities within yourself and you are able to recognize life as it is in those about you if you will just let yourself see. The only thing that prevents it is your unwillingness to drop what you have come to believe is your state or condition. Drop the veil and behold, there is the light.

7. To advance, you must come to see yourself as a Master. You must conduct yourself as a Master. There is no one who can teach you mastery nor is there anyone who can give you mastership, for they are already yours. Practice is required. You must live as a Master lives, think as a Master thinks, act like a Master acts before you would know a Master if you were to meet one.

8. Just how do you think a Master would meet the situations you have to face every day? Try meeting your problems in that same way. How would a Master speak to those about him? Try speaking in the same way. What would a Master's attitude be

toward those about him? Try expressing the same attitude. Could you imagine a Master worrying about business? Would a Master gossip and hate and become jealous or angry? Would he flinch at some particular task? Well, there is a pattern for you, for your own idea of how a Master would face life is exactly the way you should be facing it. If you will so face life, conscious that this is the determination moving in the Universe with which you are one, you will find the seeds of your own mastership sprouting and growing into their full stature.

9. Can you not certainly see that what they have always taught is true, that it is not necessary for you to sit long hours in Samadhi or go through mystical rites and religious forms to come into illumination? They have prepared the way. They have proved that when you work outside the mind with its thoughts and just enter into life as it is, you are then in the state of mastership and, by so continuing until it is your own attitude as you face life, that you are then a Master. Drop that self which you seem to be and begin to live your life as you inherently feel you should live it and you will find that to be truly YOUR life.

10. Nor is it at all necessary for you to journey to India to find your master or teacher as many students believe. Your teacher and your master is your own SELF. The Masters and Jesus do not journey in the world for their knowledge and power. They look within themselves to that Self which is the God within and that is why they are masters. So long as you seek outside of yourself that which is to be found only within yourself, you will not find it. It is in this way that you will always be able to know the teachings of a real master. The unillumined tell you that you must find some teacher outside yourself but a Master tells you that you must find the teach-

er within. This is the main point which Christ tried to make clear to the world. "Lo here and lo there" is the anti-Christ teaching. "The Father within" is the true Christ teaching.

11. It is now seen what you find moving in your Self, that deepest side of your own nature, you must be doing outwardly. Practice makes perfect and it is by practicing your own Mastership or living life as it should be lived, doing as you instinctively feel a Master would be doing, that you will find that all you have been seeking is already here, completely manifest. All that was necessary was that you completely step out of character as you have been living and into the new character, living as life should be lived.

12. When one learns to live from the Soul, the Self, and not from the mind, everything in life is clear and understandable. You know what you should do, where you should go, and life becomes simple and harmonious. That is life as it is intended, life as it is, life as we must ultimately live it. Children only live in the realm of thought when we have taught them to do so. They live naturally in the beginning and we should become like them and not make them over like ourselves. That does not mean we shall live unintelligent lives and that we will have no thoughts. It means that we will truly live intelligently and that our thoughts will be the outcome of properly expressing the Inner Self.

13. It is true, to make this complete change from what we appear to be to what we really are, to enter into life as it is, will require some determination. Whatever the Hindu's belief is, he gives his all for it. He will walk hundreds of miles to fulfill what he believes to be his spiritual duty. When we are equally intent upon being what we instinctively feel we should be, we shall arrive without difficulty. We

must quit hoping and wishing and set about doing and being.

THE CORRESPONDENT WRITES

Note: Because of the interest and helpful suggestions which the following letter from Mrs. Grace G. Hahn will hold for the students, we are making it a part of the lesson at this time. Mrs. Hahn was a member of the party with Mr. Spalding in India.

"I will try to recount some of the experiences since writing you last.

"Mr. M. M. Ghose, a friend of Mr. Spalding's, invited us to be his guests on a river boat trip to Dacca, the Ashram of Swami Paramananda. It would be very difficult to describe the jungle through which we passed. At places the river was so narrow that it was impossible for two boats to pass. Then again the river was one-half mile in width. All was going well as we proceeded on our journey. On the evening of the third day at eight-fifteen, most of us were asleep in our bunks when we felt a terrific impact and heard loud screaming close by. We soon realized we had collided with another steamer. Suffice it to say that confusion and terror reigned for some little time and we were informed that the barge of the other steamer sank in a few moments. We were damaged but no lives were lost. It was impractical to proceed so we anchored for the night. The lights were gone and the boats were leaking badly. The small son of our host calmly entered the circle of excitement on deck and said: 'God has saved us all, Baba (father), now can I go to bed'? There was a hush for a few moments; then we all realized the lesson which this blessed Hindu boy had given us. We quietly went to our beds with the assurance that all was well. Here was a potential Master, quieting a whole boatload of people by his calm assurance and simple childlike faith.

"The next morning we proceeded slowly to the next town and took the train back to Calcutta. We are meeting some very wonderful Hindu men. A Mr. Sircar presented his book to Mr. Spalding and may I quote a single paragraph from the book which appealed to me? 'Complete Truth and life in its finest flowering cannot be enjoyed unless all the forces; natural and spiritual, can be controlled and applied to the unfolding of life in its increasing fineness.' We have spent many, many hours with him and feel greatly enriched thereby.

"A story told us at the Calcutta University one afternoon is well worth mentioning for the lesson it carries. The incident occurred 600 B. C. Even in those days there were disagreements in the teachings, so part of the adherents separated from the main group and tried to persuade the teacher to change his viewpoint. After a period of time the leader of the withdrawing faction saw that it was useless and decided to take the law into his own hands. He laid in ambush and when the teacher passed him he drew his sword. As the wounded teacher fell he called the assailant to him and asked him to sit by his side for a moment as he wished with his last gasping breath to speak to him. Very kindly and lovingly he told him to go straight ahead and then no one would know what had happened and thus many people be saved from avenging his death because in reality he was going on to a greater realization, but that if he returned the way he came he would cause many others to suffer for his deed. He alone would suffer for the crime which was his. The great Master gave this lesson to the man who thought he could harm him.

"We left Calcutta last Monday and arrived at the Ashram of Swami Omkar. Such a wonderful restful place in the country thirty miles from the railroad. After a couple of days of rest, each one of us was called individually to interview the Swami. As I sat listening to him talk in his quiet, calm voice I saw the light glow all around him and back of him. I was spellbound for a few moments and was afraid it would disappear but it remained as long as I did. The room was aglow just as Mr. Spalding has told us many times. It was my first actual experience and one that I shall always cherish and remember.

"Last evening I was again privileged to spend two hours with the Swami. He explained in detail the meaning of masters, or mastership. Masters become masters of themselves first. Mastery over anger, jealousy, greed, egotism, possessions — the wife possessing the husband and the husband possessing the wife — selfishness, and a thousand other things which we have taken upon ourselves.

"We came thousands of miles to see a master, one who has accomplished that which we could and must do in our own homes and environment. Just like the cow that wants the grass on the other side of the fence even though there is abundance all around. Swami gives one word as the foundation upon which we start upon the path and that is PRACTICE. Practice daily that which you already know. Practice mastery over anger. Practice the mastery of love toward everything in the Universe. A very large order I grant you but by eternal practice hourly and daily we will soon see the results and thus be ready for another lesson in the school of life. These silent men know the value of the law of mastery over the self and thus they do not mingle with those that have not yet learned to be silent for at least some part of each day. How can we ever hope to contact them in our western chaotic state of mind? Argument shuts the door. An open mind and intuition alone throw the portals wide open. This much I have so far learned in India. I thought I knew it before but, when you come into the presence of one of these Holy men, you very soon realize it was theoretical only. It requires the actual practice and the soul's sincere desire to master the self and really become that which *they* have become.

"There is a wonderful Hindu boy here twelve years of age. He is a little master in the making. He anticipates every want or desire before we are able to express it. The eyes are the windows of the soul, therefore one must see the radiance of that youngster's smile as he silently stands before you wanting to serve you. He stood at my door last night and seemed reluctant to depart. Not yet accustomed to the Hindu custom, I waited for him to make his wants known and, as he advanced toward me with that wonderful smile, he looked me straight in the eye and said, 'I love you so.' Then he turned and was gone like a flash. During the meditation class he sits immovable for an hour in the silence. Some of the older ones go to sleep but not this child.

"We spent one happy week with the Swami, then wended our way southward to Madras. Mr. Spalding went ahead to Tiruvannamali and met Paul Brunton, the author of 'The Secret Search of India.' Mr. Spalding wired us to come and after a night's journey we were met by Mr. Spalding and Mr. Brunton. We were taken to the ashram of one of the greatest living saints in India: Sri Ramana Maharishi. A great many people sit on the floor cross-legged for many hours just to be in the presence of this great man. He is one of the Holy men who gives his time to the students. He never speaks unless a question is asked and before the answer is given he remains silent until the answer comes from within. This contact alone is worth the whole trip.

"From Tiruvannamali we went to Pondicherry. A great man lives here but only appears in public three times a year. The next time will be on the twenty-fourth of February. The ashram is one to be long remembered. Many, many men students are living there and one is greatly attracted to them. Their faces radiate the life they live and there is absolutely no doubt about it. From here we learned that a Mela, or pilgrimage, would take place in Allahabad on the thirteenth of January. We went to Calcutta and then on to Allahabad. Never will I forget the sight which we saw at this Mela. Pilgrims from all over India, coming to bathe in the sacred waters of the Ganges, were there. The confluence of these two rivers, Ganges and Jumna, occurs here. The water is icy cold, yet they plunge in. They have come long distances under terrible hardships to join in this religious rite. A million people with but one thought, namely to bathe in the Ganges on this par-ticular day. There were so many incongruous 'get ups.' Some naked, others bordering on savagery; some on elephants and camels, others in ox carts, all headed for the Ganges. I was greatly impressed by the religious zeal evidenced beyond question of doubt. What was it that would impel a million people to come to the Ganges? It was beyond my comprehension and the question seemed to revolve in my mind over and over. 'What am I seeking for in this place?' After I returned to the hotel the answer seemed to come and it was this: 'You are seeking the Primal cause of brotherhood.' How can you be one with all mankind if you see only the exterior, if you think they are psychopathic pa-tients; if you say that black is black and white is white? Do you not observe the same love throbbing in the heart of the mother as she fondles her babe whose tiny body is filthy, diseased, and crippled, wallowing in the dirt, poverty stricken, homeless, and actually starving, walking miles under tremendous hardships merely to bathe in the 'sacred' waters of the Ganges? What but the inborn spark of Divinity could possibly urge them on to lay it all at the feet of their conception of God? We worship God in luxury; they have nothing. Their feet are weary and footsore, their energy is their all, yet they give it to come once a year and every six, twelve and twenty-four years to meet on common ground and bathe and worship in their way. Just think of it. A million people on a small area of ground, peaceable, happy, singing and joyous. No sign of confusion or interference, each one regarding the rights of his brother to worship as he pleases.

"To me the real brotherhood is expressed here under inconceivable conditions, thousands of conditions which we never thought could exist and yet, from the hearts of these pilgrims love is expressed and the eyes reveal an unfathomable depth which we might well envy. All worshiping God, God, God. Many different languages, the rich and the poor, the halt, the lame and the blind. A smile will always bring forth a smile. In fact, they seem surprised that we will deign to smile or greet them in their own fashion. I sincerely wonder if we would smile under the same environment. Could we, or would we, on hands and knees crawl to the Ganges, worshipping God with every breath, scarcely able to keep soul and body together? Could we, I ask you, could we?

"We saw Saddus with matted hair, their bodies covered with ashes, naked with the exception of a G-string, and I asked the question, 'why should anyone treat the body in such a fashion?' The answer was that they have relinquished pride and are no longer concerned with the world. That is their conception of it and, after all is said and done, we all act and think as our conscience dictates and as our individual evolution has progressed.

"We take pride in 'dolling up' the body, while they go to the other extreme and spend their entire lives in caves and in the Himalayan mountains in the contemplation of God. They must first realize these attributes in themselves before they can go into the world and teach their inner experiences to others. We have many isms, creeds, and dogmas very often theoretical and intellectual only. Thousands of these pilgrims coming in from all over India for this great Mela are actually living the God-life as they understand it. Of course there are many professional beggars and one soon learns to differentiate. The intuition is the best guide. Beggars are beggars whether they are in India or in America. Here we see them in the 'raw' and there we often meet them in the best of society.

"We witnessed a man returning from the Ganges walking with a cane, his servant just behind him carrying his crutches. You may draw your own conclusions.

"Another great day is just ahead. On Friday the twenty-fourth the Mela of the sixth year occurs, so we will remain for that. I will continue this letter after that occasion. Mr. Spalding has taken two of our party to the Ganges today. I have remained at home to get this letter off to you."

GRACE G. HAHN

168

FOR THE TEACHER

In presenting this chapter, the letter from Mrs. Hahn should be read to the class, as it completely illustrates the lesson. Incident by incident, which the tour party experienced, is explained in the lesson and the teacher can readily check from the lesson to the illustrations in the letter.

Paragraph 1. The age-old illustration of the child is not that we become feeble-minded or that we lack intelligence. It means that we live life as it moves out from our interior nature. That is why it is difficult for children to understand adults. They have not had their minds filled with thoughts and they only live what they inwardly feel. When these inner feelings are completely dulled by having our thoughts drilled into them children become dull and inefficient like the older people. Thought is not the leading factor in successful living but is the outcome of successful living. Every step in human progress came from some one's inner conviction and thought was evolved to describe that which has been achieved.

Paragraph 2. Man is really not limited at all for he is a replica of infinity. He only allows himself to be limited by his thought. Live life as it unfolds from within and you will find life as it is and the key to your own mastership. Thought, word, and act are the outlets or vehicles through which life is expressed and not the standard from which it is lived.

Paragraphs 3 and 4. The purpose of the Universe is to perpetuate and perfect life in all its completeness. It supports in man only that which is in harmony with life. It destroys out of man's nature that which operates against life. It is said that evil bears the seed of its own destruction and that is true but

169

the seed of destruction in evil is the inherent good and when good manifests it destroys evil, leaving nothing but the good. And life is the good that is always present and always moving to fulfill itself.

Paragraph 5. It is not an intelligent thing to place blame upon yourself or upon others. The only true intelligent thing to do is to protect yourself and others from anything that is less than the Universal divinity. When we become as intent upon preserving the potential nature of ourselves and others as we are intent upon preserving our earthly possessions, the world will be filled with real Masters.

Paragraph 6. Look at yourself in the mirror. Is there any light in your face when you are sad? When you are radiant with joy, is there a light there? Imagine the light which would emanate from you if you were living that kind of life which you idealize and which is your life as you are capable of living it and as you should live it.

Paragraphs 7, 8 and 9. "If you want to know God, act as though God were."

If you want to know what the life of a master is like, live that life yourself. Only in this way can we really know. No man knows the things of God except the spirit of God, which is in him, shall reveal them.

Paragraphs 10 and 11. The distinct difference between the teachings of the illumined and the unillumined is that the illumined teach you to go within yourself for knowledge. All the rest go and teach others to seek, outside themselves. You are not likely to find outside of yourself what you have failed to find within yourself. The world gives back to you what you give into the world.

Paragraph 12. One should study the difference between the state of his mind and the state of his soul. The mind says thus and so and that only this and that are possible. The soul knows itself to be immortal, to be the Master, and it never changes in its activity. Your deepest desire is identical with the manner in which any Master would act.

Paragraph 13. Complete devotion to an ideal is the secret of its attainment. It is not wishing and hoping for things to break right but persistently working toward the goal of perfection.

CHAPTER XII

PRANA

1. It is a well known fact today that the Cosmic Life Force surrounds and interpenetrates every condition and every atom and that the Life Force can be drawn within our bodies with the breath we breathe. Every act can be according to that Life Force. Every thought we think can be in harmony with it.

2. Note that it is said that this Life Force may be drawn in "with the breath we breathe." It is not the mere act of breathing that draws into the body of man this Cosmic Life Force. Unless definite attention to it accompanies our physical breathing it is not definitely appropriated. It is a life force which is so much finer than our physical air that it is not affected by mere physical processes any more than one might draw electricity into his being by the mere act of physical breathing. Of course there is a certain amount of electricity, or what we call electricity, that is taken into the system by every act and, likewise, with the Cosmic Life Force which is sometimes called Prana. If you will notice, everything toward which your attention is directed registers an impression on the mind. In turn, this impression is developed into an idea and the idea expressed in words. This is a sort of mental breathing, is it not? Well, there is an inner attention, a deep longing you call it, to be perfect in every department of your being. When the outer attention is linked with this inner attention or when it looks always toward the perfection of the Universe, as does what Seneca called the "eye of the soul," then

there is drawn into man's being the elements of the Cosmic forces around and about us. The mystics have always taught that attention is the secret of success in dealing with the Cosmic forces. Deep, sincere, abiding attention to the surrounding spiritual ethers, a completely relaxed body and an all-absorbing interest and complete openness of mind are the necessary attitudes in order that one may realize this "inner breath" as it is called. This is "soul breathing" or letting the Self expand into its native ethers, the interpenetrating life force or spiritual ethers, as Steinmetz called it, until through the act of attention it is drawn within the whole being of man.

3. This Life Force being Cosmic must interpenetrate all elements. This is, in reality, the force that stimulates all cellular growth, allows it to expand and become the growth of the body as well as the growth of plants. In fact, it is incorporated with all growth of every description and is the sustaining element of life. It becomes that which imbibes life as well for, like every other force, it is both positive and negative and acts and reacts within itself, just as whirling currents of air act and react within themselves. One might say that the air breathes, or moves and, at the same time, is acting within itself and upon itself.

4. The method of consciously appropriating the universal Cosmic Life Force, or Prana, is commonly called Pranayama. One might call it Prana-breathing or the practice of consciously breathing the Cosmic Life Force. The exact procedure is difficult to define and it would take too much time and space to give the entire technique of the Pranic breath. The technique for starting the operation is proper breathing, then one may with care and sincerity find his own method for the balance of the process.

As we have said above, attention is the one fundamentally important practice in the process — attention to the highest source of energy existing, that all-surrounding presence that you call God. The mind must be without strain and whatever method best relieves the mind of strain would be the next step in right procedure. In fact, the Prana or spiritual substance is so fine and sensitive that it is deflected by the least force. Did you ever try to catch a piece of lint or down floating in the air? Every tense or quick movement to grasp it only drove it away but a quietness that was like letting it come between your fingers of its own volition was the proper technique for grasping it. That is as nearly an illustration as one could give. It is also like trying to remember something you have forgotten. If you make strong mental effort you do not remember but, if you let the mind rest, become quietly reflective, then the idea comes quickly within the mind. So with the Prana, it is breathed into the nature through quietness and confidence. Every phase of the mind must be free and the body completely relaxed. One must have a sense of complete freedom and complete expansion as if the cells of the body were actually moving out from each other until they almost stood apart. This practice may be continued until one forgets the sense of physical limitation altogether, then one is in the most perfect state mentally and physically to receive this Universal Substance into his whole being. It then has access to every cell of his being; it becomes the sustaining and invigorating element of life and especially of the human body. This method of control causes the body to keep young and vibrant.

5. It is a sustaining and invigorating practice that allows the cells and tissues of the body to expand, thereby giving greater oxidation to the body.

It is a complete spiritual airing of every cell of the body to the original ethers from which it came. Just as in a ray of light you find the various colors, so in Prana do you find all the elements of life, that is the real essence of all the lesser forces. Prana is not oxygen but is that which gives life to the oxygen, the actual life within the oxygen. It is that which gives force to electricity, consciousness to mind. In other words, it is the reality existing within and standing back of and sustaining all lesser forces. It is called the Spirit of God in the Scriptures. Pranayama—spiritual breathing—allows the proper expansion of all the elements taken into the body for the body's growth and, because of this expansion, all the elements are oxidized or "aired" as we say when we expose things to the air or sun to become freshened. Just so when the body is relaxed, when the mind and spirit are freed, when the whole nature expands to consciously allow the Prana to interpenetrate throughout the entire being, the whole nature is freshened, revived, refreshed, fed. This is Pranayama or the art of spiritual breathing. But, attention is the fundamental secret of the practice. You even have to give attention to the sun in order to gain the greatest benefit from a sun bath.

6. It is through this practice that certain Yogi are able to suspend animation for certain periods of time. This rests the whole system and renews it for the contact with its origin or source. It is restored and the original life elements are again contacted by the flesh itself. In the same way and, with the same results, they suspend respiration. It is like coming up out of the water into fresh air after one has been submerged for a period. To try to suspend animation and respiration would only be to drown yourself literally. But, to expand yourself and so relax yourself that you begin to consciously sense the

life-giving ethers, makes one so much alive, so vitally filled with life, so refreshed and fed that one has no need of the outer breath or the outer activities of the body. He becomes alive from within.

7. Just as this practice vitalizes the body, so it enlivens the mind. The reason men do not think well is because the mind is too tense, too compressed — so to speak — so that it does not function freely. Under the practice of Pranayama the whole nature is expanded and functions more freely and completely. It is like loosening bearings that are too tight on a machine and letting the oil penetrate through it. It then moves more freely. Memory, in this case, comes in from a thousand different sources and one remembers what he was in the beginning. It comes without any effort at all and anything he wants to know comes instantly and easily into his mind. Inasmuch as Prana interpenetrates all, there must be a close relationship between Prana and that function of the mind. Prana allows no division in function for it unites all the functions of the individual with the Universal. It is, of course, Universal and opens the way for all activities, thousands and thousands of activities at the same time. Prana is an emanating energy underlying all substance. Of course, substance in its original state is energy and energy is substance. What we know as energy and substance are but two aspects of a single primal energy and this primal energy is Prana, or Spirit.

8. We may more truly say that Prana is one of the elements of Spirit for spirit is not only energy but intelligence and substance. It is more subtle than ether. The Western World is defining ether as Prana, though there is a difference in the subtlety and the activity of Prana and ether. The latter is nascent while Prana is always active. Ether is Prana becoming or coming out toward manifestation. All

of the finer forces of nature such as electricity and the other moving elements of creation are divisions and mediums in which and through which Prana works.

9. When the human body or any material form disintegrates it goes back into Prana, first into the various forms of energy and thence back into Universal and primal force. If Prana were constantly received into the whole being of man, the flesh would be eternally quickened, or it would become more and more animated, more and more alive, and the last enemy would be overcome. There are those who overcome old age and death with or through an understanding of Prana right along. They rebuild the body with the Pranic influence. This happens in a slight degree every time one goes to sleep or rests but, when one adds conscious attention to the Pranic Presence, completely relaxes in mind and body, the attention breathes the ever-present Prana into and through his whole being; therefore, the greatest degree of renewal of mind and body is attained.

10. You see, intelligence is the primal attribute of being and the activity of consciousness is Prana, or vital force of creation, and substance is the form through which both act. Intelligence, Life, and Substance are the trinity of elements in the first cause as defined by the Western world. Intelligence is its KNOWING aspect. Life is its QUICKENING or vital aspect. Substance is the aspect which has the capacity of FORM. Prana is usually used as embracing both the substance and life elements and they are the vehicles or mediums through which intelligence moves to direct and determine the created forms.

11. This primal intelligence, life, and substance are just God Almighty in action but it must become

a conscious fact in every individual. It becomes selective to the individual and is of conscious use to the individual as the individual selects it.

12. The Cosmic Ray of which Millikan speaks is a Pranic wave. They will find nine divisions of the Cosmic ray which are all definitely Pranic in origin. They can be of great benefit if properly used. These nine rays are the emanations of Pranic energy, just as the seven colors are emanations of a ray of pure white light. Creation is only the splitting up and recombining of influences or energies, as we call them, emanating from the Pranic ethers.

13. When we go back to the center of anything, it is pure light and this is the inner light of which Jesus spoke. It is the light of Illumination. The greater man's spiritual awakening, the greater the light. Have you not noticed that one awakened in joy has a radiance about his countenance? When one is spiritually awake, the light is correspondingly bright. That is why artists paint Jesus with a halo of light about him. Light is life. This is the "light that lighteth every man that cometh into the world" and it is the fire through which the initiates of the occult schools had to walk in order to be eligible to illumination. This light is all about us and is an emanation of the Pranic ethers. It is the light which is the beginning and the end of creation. When you can live in the light, as you now live in your sense of body, you will be immortal for the light never dies. I was noticing a report of some kind of light shining in Transjordan although archaeologists were perfectly sure that there was nothing there of an old civilization. Those following the light found and broke into archaeological remains very quickly. That has happened in Persia as well. We have not yet seen it in the Gobi. There is a history, however, that the light always showed in

that country. We have a complete history, in fact, that that light showed over the first tower of Babel, a tower that was built of actual stone in the form of a step-pyramid. However, this light is seen only through the Single Eye, such devoted attention that all the senses and faculties of man are pointed in one direction and that direction must be toward what the Scriptures call the "light of His countenance."

14. `This is the light of the New Jerusalem spoken of by John in Revelations. John knew well how to use the Pranic Light. He extended his vision to take in all of it. It is, of course, much beyond what we know as clairvoyance, though clairvoyance is a phase of it and is really a step backward in evolution. It is like living in the borrowed light from another when the true light, the light that lighteth every man, is within him.

15. We must go forward to that Light and the lower senses which hold us back or away from our birthright will let go. The limited activities direct us away from the unfoldment and use of the Pranic Light by the higher sense. The psychic faculties will fall into line and become valuable instruments when the Pranic Light is unfolded. The Pranic light vibrates way beyond the psychic forces. Furthermore, mediumship and so-called psychic development are not steps toward the unfoldment of the direct Pranic Light.

16. Pranic light can always be called upon to overcome any degrading forces that oppose it, just as light can be brought into play to dispel darkness. It can be the I AM center. The statement, "I am the force of that Pranic Light and I project It and put it forth as all powerful," will break that condition of the conflicting forces or voices every time. But it must be the voice of the Christ Self, which is

the real I AM within each individual. This I AM is not above you or outside of you but at the very center of your being. That was Jesus' thought when he said, "I have nothing except that which comes in the Name and through the Power of the Christ." It involves the highest embodiment of Prana.

17. The transfiguration of Christ was when the consciousness of Jesus was merged into the realization that Intelligence, Life, and Substance were in the last analysis ONE and that One was what he called the Father, or primal cause, like all the various colors of the spectrum returning to a pure ray of white light.

18. There is but one Consciousness, One Principle, One Sense. It is only complicated when we deal too much with differentiations or apparently differing functions and attributes. To deal with the mind as functioning in many faculties is only to further dissipate yourself and draw you further and further away from your source. Behold, our God is ONE. With that one thought, or attitude, of Pranic forces always being in operation within as well as about us, we become unified, or one with the whole. John said that that which is without is really within. He carried it right to that great Pranic force which always exists and is always active and this action is the One action throughout all creation and all space.

FOR THE TEACHER

The foregoing lesson received from Mr. Spalding by the India Tour party deals with a subject most vital to every student. It reveals the close relationship which exists in the minds of the Hindoo Scientists of Calcutta University and other Eastern scientists and the religion of the Orient. We are fast approaching the time when walls of difference are to be entirely dissolved and the ultimate union of religion and science will be generally recognized as one and the same thing, though they may often approach a single fact from opposite directions.

Paragraph 1. In the matter of successful living it should be clearly understood that man is not sustained by what he has commonly considered essential. His real supply must necessarily be contained within the movement of forces which operated to create him in the beginning. Within these forces are all the elements out of which the visible creation is formed and it is only through a conscious contact with these original forces that man may hope to successfully live life to its fullest possibilities.

Paragraph 2. The "Cosmic breath" is not a matter of physical breathing but it is a matter of conscious contact with the Life forces that move in the spiritual ethers about us. Breathing is receiving into your nature the elements within the air, and then exhaling what the body does not assimilate. Spiritual breathing is receiving into the consciousness of man that which is within the spiritual ethers and that is brought about through the quiet and deep attention of the mind. People often related it to physical breathing, but it should not be confused with this process. Whatever you look upon, you receive impressions concerning it into the consciousness and everything you do is an expression of what thus impresses you. By attention to the spiritual ethers you draw their elements into your being and your whole life's expression is quickened and increased because of the very nature of that which occupies your attention.

Paragraph 3. One should contemplate the permeating presence of all the forces of Being until he becomes as conscious of these forces as he is now conscious of form. This is the secret of developing unlimited power or mastery.

Paragraph 4. Pranic breath is not something mystical or difficult and does not require a lot of instruction. One easily and readily absorbs the sunshine for it is the nature of sunlight to penetrate all objects upon which it shines. More penetrating is the vital energies of the spiritual ethers. Relaxed, quiet attention is the secret.

Paragraph 5. Physical tension is a contraction of the flesh caused by mental contractions. Mental contractions are caused by studying the apparent limitations of form and environment. A wider view of life frees the mind which in turn frees the body. Give your whole being a good pranic airing every day and watch the increase in every capacity of your being.

Paragraph 6. Suspended animation is not a matter of merely stopping the processes of bodily functions. It is identifying one's self with a superior action that meets all the requirements of the physical being; then the so-called normal functions are not necessary. The greater always supersedes the lesser and fulfills the needs of the lesser. Do not try to stop eating or breathing or cause the heart to stop. Apply yourself to the Divine presence until you find it quickening your entire being.

Paragraph 7. Vitality or living energy is not the result of food or breath. It is the activity of the life force of the Universe re-animating the being of man.

Paragraph 8. Spirit is the activity of the entire creative machinery of the Universe; it is God in action. This action involves all the elements within the nature of God and, therefore, contains all the elements involved in creation.

Paragraph 9. Death and decay is only a lack of animation from the source of one's being as is failure and poverty.

Paragraphs 10 and 11. The Universal Cause knows what it is doing and it knows what you should be doing to fulfill its purposes. Constant attentiveness to all the activities of the Spirit is to know and to have the power to do.

Paragrphs 12 and 13. Light is life but there are higher forms of light just as there are higher forms of ether and energy. Only the individual who practices the Presence of God can know exactly what that light is like but one who is given to deep meditation often catches a glimpse of it.

Paragraph 14. True clairvoyance—clear vision—is not seeing shapes and forms but is that awareness of mind that sees and knows the pure action of Spirit.

Paragraph 15. Do not wait to do what you call overcoming before you feel worthy to enter the path that leads to illumination. Go into the light and let it burn away that which is false. Drop your faults, diseases, undesirable conditions. Face the light and these conditions are not.

Paragraphs 16 and 17. Pranic light, or Spiritual light, is not something difficult to obtain any more than is physical light. It is always moving toward you and works as quickly through your highest ideals or least needs with infinite swiftness just as physical light flashes instantly through any opening large or small.

Paragraph 18. Reducing everything to oneness simplifies the entire matter of living and spiritual progress.

CHAPTER XIII

THE QUANTUM THEORY

1. Principles of physics are involved in a study of the Quantum Theory. It is the theory of distribution of energy throughout nature. It was developed in the Berlin University as an outcome of investigation into radiation from black objects. This research resulted in the conclusion that all forms radiate a definite energy and that there is nothing in the world of form that is an inert mass. Every form has within itself some degree of energy and this energy is a distinct emanation of the energy that fills infinite space. The amount of energy that each particular form radiates is in direct proportion to the relationship which it has with the Universal energy.

2. Just as a pendulum swings in a long or short arc according to the amount of force exerted to start it swinging, just so all forms retain the amount of active energy required in sending it forth. This energy is retained by the form just to the degree that it retains its relation to the energy which sent it forth. If the pendulum stops, it is because the impelling force has ceased to exert influence upon it. Matter becomes less and less active as it loses some of its contact with the original impelling force which started it into motion. When this energy ceases to act within the form, the form disintegrates.

3. Metaphysically, this has much of vital importance to those of the Western world. The movement in the United States came under the depression and all that that means is that there was no foundation

in fact. That is, it was founded on only a half truth. There is fact as a basis for our metaphysics but that fact was overlooked and misunderstood by most of its exponents in the United States. This will all be discussed in our consideration of the Quantum Theory.

4. The Eastern world, those of higher thought, have known the facts propounded in the Quantum Theory. They deal, in brief, with but one fact, that of the universality of all things and, consequently, in dealing with that one fact they have a definite basis for both science and metaphysics. The psychology of the Western world is mere child's play. It is based to a great extent upon theory. Whenever you deal with divisions of mental, material, and physical you are bound to base at least 75% of your calculations on theory. Division is not unity and unity is not division and the basis of all creation is that it is a unit. "I am that I am and beside me there is no other," is the eternal declaration of fact which is the unity of all things. The direct violation of this fundamental unity is in considering the mind as having phases or faculties, when, in reality, mind is a single unit, not only as within the individual but as existing in and of the Universe. Material form is not something isolated from and independent of the Universe but is one in and with the Universal substance. The physical body is not an isolated phase of the creative scheme but is in and one with the Universal Energy. To violate this fundamental unity is to isolate yourself in a hypnotic state where you seem to be a separate being and, therefore, you cut yourself off, devitalize yourself, and ultimately destroy your ability to further manifest in this plane. To deny the relationship of the visible with the invisible is to push yourself right out of your body and into the invisible.

5. The Eastern philosophy is not based upon theory at all. It is based upon a definite scientific fact or principle. That is the same idea that Einstein is bringing out in the Quantum Theory. He has brought it out in greater evidence than has any other scientist in the Western world. Many are saying that it is the gap between Science or Physics and true Religious thought.

6. The Easterner does not approach the matter of religious thought as theory at all. In fact, he proves that it is not theory. Thereby, he accomplishes that very fact and the possibilities involved in that fact. You do not see the Eastern philosophers pass out a theory of anything. Their basis is always in fact. It, of course, is not fact simply because they pronounce it so but because it has a scientific basis in fact. That fact was clearly revealed by Christ when he said, "I and my father are ONE," preserving the unity of himself with the whole. That is the basis from which all successful living must evolve and it is only to the degree that this oneness is maintained by the individual that he begins to radiate the energy that sent him into being. This is the basis of the Quantum Theory as applied from the viewpoint of pure religion or pure metaphysics. And that is why the Eastern philosophers gave so much attention to the Quantum Theory. They see the scientists of the world returning to the basis of their own religious thought held for thousands of years.

7. Einstein did not come right out and say that it is all Spirit. Consequently, it was urged that the physical or material was not a fact, but he showed that it is based upon one joint determination. He put it as one general Principle, co-relating all physics, as he said, under one head. That is exactly what

those of higher Eastern thought had determined long ago—that there is but one Principle, one scientific basis, and that basis one of Being.

8. Now the Western world does not go back and reason from that Principle. They work through to that principle from the external, consequently it is not necessarily a true form of reasoning; that is, their form of reason is not truly scientific reason. All true reason works out from principle to its manifestation and not from the manifestation back to principle. Imagine trying to work a problem by reasoning back or attempting to reason back to Principle by studying the size, shape, form and general construction of an accumulation of figures. The people of the Western world, in their attempt to solve the riddle of life, are doing that very thing. By this process they become highly mental or, as we put it, intellectual. And as we already know, their intellectual knowledge is always subject to revision for it does not prove itself. That is why one of our modern scientists has said that all written works on science prior to the last ten years should be burned. The Eastern world is carried beyond the intellectual or the ordinary intellectual. Of course, true principle and reason from the basis of the One Fact is the highest form of intellect. But the hypothesis that the Eastern world takes puts it wholly on a true intellectual basis in carrying it to a clear conception.

9. The intellect of the Western world covers a wide range but comes to no absolute conclusion in its hypotheses or theories. All of the Science of the Western world has been based upon that hypothesis or theory. The people of the Western world have progressed to the point where they know the existence of certain determining factors but they never go directly to the simple denominator of One Prin-

ciple when handling fact. The Eastern philosophers have always based their premises upon one Natural Fact. And there you have the basis of the Quantum Theory. One Universal Fact from which all form emanates and operates as the animating force of the created form — the Universal distribution of energy.

10. The difference between the Hindu conception and the theory of Monism is that the latter eliminated all but the blind force of nature or creation. The Hindu always considered it an active, intelligent force that knew what it was doing, an energetic force, and a force that did accomplish an intelligent creation that moved toward an intelligent purpose and that anyone who would work with the intelligence of that force could accomplish all things through it.

11. The crux of the whole matter is therefore right knowledge. What we have called knowledge is past. The true knowledge is outside of the senses. The true basis of knowledge is to know the motivating force and the ends toward which it moves, as it is this motivating sense or the inward sense of the trend of the motivating force of the Universe that brought all things into existence in the beginning and will bring all things into being through that individual who senses and works in harmony with its purpose.

12. The true knowledge comes through samadhi or silence. It comes through an inner feeling or an intuitive knowing. This is rightly what we call understanding. With all your getting, get understanding. When we obey what we inwardly feel the accomplishment is achieved and then we have correct knowledge for it is based on the outworking of Principle. This is the manner in which all true knowledge comes, not only in things spiritual, but in rela-

tion to the principles which we use every day. We discover certain principles, apply those principles, results are forthcoming, and from these results we formulate our knowledge.

13. When you take that knowledge completely out of the realm of hypnosis you get down to the fundamental fact or truth. Knowledge does not necessarily exist in the fundamental fact. That fact exists prior to and is greater than knowledge. Knowledge, as the Hindu puts it, comes directly from the expression of the fundamental fact.

14. When the Bible says that "the flesh profiteth nothing" it does not say that the flesh is nothing. It has no reality except that which is of the Spirit which produced it. The flesh is not a producer; it does not produce anything for it is the thing produced. It is the Spirit which produces. Flesh is Spirit in form, as they put it. They do not make any distinction between flesh and Spirit or material and spiritual. Consequently, it is all one and the same to them and that is where they accomplish. The Word made flesh is the true spiritual form.

15. When the Spirit works in manifest form it obeys a manifestation of law. If you can know that Law you can know Spirit definitely. As Paul says, "Faith is Spirit substance." It means that Faith, made knowing, is all substance. You know instead of having Faith. There is where the Sanskrit never deviates. That evidence of Spirit, which is first faith and then knowing, creates. Through that evidence men create always, not through the senses or the sense of the material or physical, but through all substance as Spirit.

16. Faith is the active principle of the mind. The mind acting upon inner knowing or understanding ripens into knowledge or becomes absolute knowl-

189

edge. Spiritual intuition is direct knowing; it is tapping the infinite consciousness directly at its source. This power of direct knowing is born in every individual. Some manifest it earlier in life, chiefly because they are less hypnotized. That is, the less one is subjected to the supposed knowledge of the race, which is really ignorance, the more readily does that one follow what he instinctively knows and feels to be true. It is within the individual always and must be brought out.

17. Jesus said, "I have nothing save that which comes in the name and through the power of Christ," putting himself in direct receptivity to spiritual intuition at all times. What Jesus did was really a lesson in how each man should proceed in every phase of life. That you might be one with the Father even as he was one with the Father, and his contact was always through the Christ, the Word of God, that is the inner fact of all men. "Christ is all and in all" and Christ is the inner reality of each individual.

18. There is only one kind of intuition just as there is only one kind of physical sight. You can, through your eyes, look toward and discover anything you wish. You may look for beauty and ugliness and you use the same sight. One is desirable and the other is undesirable. You may train your intuition to search out the determining principle and its operations; you can train it into psychic planes and find out what is going on there; or you can train it on your neighbor and discover his secret thought and motives. But, intuition turned in any other direction than to discover the operations of the Principle itself is perversion of this sense back of all senses and hypnosis is the result, for it clouds the clear perception of the individual. The only way to

escape any degree of hypnosis is to train the intuition into the channels of direct knowing. This is the path of light and any perversion of the intuitive sense is the path of darkness.

19. The old theory of occultism that the senses must be destroyed or killed or reversed is not in accordance with the teachings of the pure Hindu philosophy. They say that all is Spirit, that the senses are Spirit but must be so used and their true spiritual significance preserved. They become avenues of expression of that which the intuition learns as coming from the Spirit. This direct knowing is also direct manifestation. If we would accept the fact which is revealed in Principle, that fact would become immediately manifest to us. It is just that easy. The Westerner has simply submerged it in complexities.

20. When you rightly understand the nature of what you call matter as pure Spirit substance, then you can see just why this is true. The Hindu says, "Compress the cube and you have a different substance. Expand it and you have a different substance." You do not define this as material or physical substance, as in the compression or expansion you do not change its nature, but only the relative position of the atoms. Water or ice is just as much H_2O, regardless of its form, and this power of expansion and contraction is the fourth dimension of it. Likewise, the power of extending anything from one magnitude to another by the simple rearrangement of the atoms is its fourth dimension and does not change its inherent character. If all things are made of Spiritual substance, there is no dividing line between what we have called Spirit and its manifestation. Only when man is under a state of hypnosis does he imagine that there is something besides the unity of all things and the oneness of all things.

191

Through his state of hypnosis he imposes false influences into form and these distortions are the fabrications of his own ignorance.

FOR THE TEACHER

Paragraphs 1 and 2. The lesson to be found in this explanation of the Quantum Theory offers unusual opportunity to impress upon the mind of the individual the fact that all of his lack is due to separating himself from the original first cause. Just as a motor stops when it is disconnected from an electrical current or a light goes out when the switch is turned off, so does man cease to function in just that degree that he separates himself from the Spirit of God.

Paragraph 3. When it comes to a matter of merely manipulating the world with thought, trying to demonstrate by the use of affirmation, man sooner or later exhausts the ability to achieve. Only through deep meditation upon the oneness of all things, man's unity with God, is his power revived so that he again returns to the position of power that is rightfully his. Man of himself can do nothing. It is the Spirit that quickens and, when his mind and nature are reanimated with the Spirit, his words and acts become alive and then only does he move with power.

Paragraphs 4, 5, 6 and 7. It makes a vast difference to man whether he proceeds from a true or from an assumed or false hypothesis. The conclusions at which he arrives in his calculations depend upon the foundation or principle from which he moves. If that foundation is false, the conclusion must be false. As creation began in the great Universal Whole, man can find no substantial starting point for his own activities except from that same basis. One cannot adapt a principle to his own thought but he must adapt himself to the movement of principle and his thoughts must be evolved from that principle. In turn, his action must conform to that same principle and then, only, can he hope to have results forthcoming that are consistent with his fundamental nature.

Paragraphs 8 and 9. These paragraphs involve the difference between true and false reason, between intelligent logic and false logic. We get our minds completely reversed when we work from the external or when we work merely for external results that we imagine will suit our own idea of things. There is an established order in the Universe and only through aligning ourselves with that natural order of things can we hope for satisfactory results.

Paragraph 10. The force which designed and created the Universe could not be considered an unintelligent force or blind force moving without conscious direction. Electricity must be governed by intelligence in our everyday affairs, else we could not have light, heat, and power resulting from it. Electricity by itself is a blind force but, subjected to the control of intelligence, it produces constructive results. So all creative force of the Universe must be subjected to the direction of intelligence, else there never could have been an orderly creation.

Paragraphs 11, 12 and 13. Right knowledge comes through becoming so still that one feels within himself the movement of Universal forces, the Spirit of God. Its activity not only becomes a vitalizing influence but it awakens an understanding in the mind of man. "The inspiration of the Almighty giveth understanding." Just as you must first understand the operation of the principle of mathematics through quiet submission to the rule, so must you contemplate the action of Divine Principle until you understand its operations. Knowledge is the accumulation of ideas and true knowlege would be the result of seeing the spirit of God made manifest. Knowledge comes in the completion of a process. Understanding discerns the way toward results.

Paragraph 14. Neither mind nor matter have any power to create or to produce. The power to produce is in Mind or Spirit. It is the Spirit that quickens. Holding thoughts and driving the body only deplete the man. Life is renewed, power awakened through communion with Spirit.

Paragraphs 15 and 16. Faith is the means through which principle is discerned and applied. First, faith is resting the mind of its own activities to gain new impetus. Secondly, it is relying upon that impetus until it produces results. Faith is a sort of mental transformer whereby unaccomplished things or unmanifest powers are brought to manifestation.

Paragraph 17. The secret of Jesus' power was in his complete reliance upon what he felt moving in his deepest nature and which he called the Father within. The law of God is written in your inward parts and, to outwardly obey what is moving within is to bring the inner capacity into outer manifestation. That which moves in the deepest side of man's nature is the inward action of the Universal Principle.

Paragraph 18. Intuition is only another avenue through which consciousness may be increased. Through intuition one gains the inner facts of life. Trained to the Omniscience of God or the all-enfolding intellingence, man can understand anything or any situation from the viewpoint of absolute knowing.

194

Paragraph 19. The outer senses are outlets or avenues through which we express inward knowledge to the outward world. The outer senses should not be condemned or destroyed. In so doing you would destroy your outlets into the world. See to it that the function of your whole being lines up with the innermost tendencies of your nature until you express what you are in the sight of God.

Paragraph 20. To know the true nature of all things, not as separated or isolated divisions, but as one and the same thing in different stages of progression, is to be possessed of the power and dominion that belongs to you as a product of One First Cause.

CHAPTER XIV

RESUME

On our present tour, we have endeavored to give the student more of the actual teachings and practices of the Masters, rather than to recite the phenomena performed by them. We have not laid much stress upon our actual contacts in India but enough has been given of our travels and contacts to satisfy the minds of those persons who have wished to know something of the trip itself. Should we relate all the incidents and experiences thus far encountered, there would be no time nor space left in which to give that vital instruction that would help the student to live in his own experiences that which the masters live and prove. The average student is more interested in the philosophy and science which the masters employ. It is only through such knowledge that the individual may know how to proceed in attaining his own mastership. Furthermore, the miraculous feats and the manner in which the masters live has doubtless been sufficiently covered in the three volumes of *Life and Teaching of the Masters of the Far East.*

This trip has yielded us much of practical knowledge and it is our purpoe at this time to review the main points in order that they may stand out in the mind of the student. Thus he may have a clearly defined working basis from which to proceed in recasting his life in accordance with those motives through which the illumined have attained to mastership. Mastership is everyone's possibility but this

state is not achieved through reading, study, or the-
orizing, but by actually living the life which the
masters live.

It has been clearly stated that life lived by the
average individual is hypnotic; that is, the majority
of men and women are not living life as it was intended at all. Not one in a million feels the freedom to live what he inwardly feels he should live.
He has come under the world opinion of himself
and this opinion is what he obeys, rather than the
law of his own being. In this respect and to this
degree he is living under an hypnotic spell. He
lives under the delusion that he is a mere human
being, living in a merely material world, and only
hopes to escape it when he dies and goes to what he
calls Heaven. This is not the determination intended in the plan and purpose of life. Obedience to
one's inner nature, the expression of life as he instinctively feels it ought to be expressed, is the very
foundation of the life which the masters reveal as
the only true mode of living.

Now, the difference between the teachings and
practices of the masters and those of fakirs is that
the fakir only intensifies the hypnotic condition of
the mind. Further false and material pictures are so
impressed upon the sensitive minds of people that
they are thrown into further states of hypnosis. The
masters say, "That which seems external exists not
at all," by which they mean that it is not what
appears that is the reality of life. The reality of life
is that which moves out from the very center of one's
being. They seek in every way to clarify their minds
of world impressions and sit in long periods of Samadhi—Silence—in order that they may see clearly
that innermost trend of their nature. Then their
next attempt is to live in thought, word, and act

that movement which they have discerned within themselves. True mastery is living the instruction of the inner teacher, the inner self, and not seeking the opinions of the world.

Nor does the method of the fakirs differ in any large measure from much of the teaching and practice of the metaphysical world of the West. The gathering of thoughts from teachers and books, building them into the conscious nature of one's being, is to establish a false determination which is largely hypnotic. The mere making of one's consciousness over according to thoughts evolved by other's minds is to impose a false condition upon that individual. To manipulate the body, the affairs, or to concentrate within the body to awaken its centers or functions is only to throw the individual further out of the true determination of life and the "last state of that man is worse than the first." Instruction received from the without must be taken into the mentality and assimilated, analyzed, checked with the deepest facts of one's own inner nature in order to determine if it be true to the Self. One best consult the Self first and gain his outer knowledge thus at first hand. The first method is slow and retarding to one's progress, while the latter is swift and freeing. Notice the difference when you act according to someone's instruction and when you obey what you instinctively feel to be the right thing to do. This of itself should teach us that the way of life is from within out.

The forces of life are silent and that is the main reason for the silent nature of the masters. That is the way they keep in harmony with life itself. Even our Scriptures teach in substance that a multitude of words is not without sin. Only when we speak in harmony with what we inwardly feel do we let ourselves out into complete harmony with the true determination of life. Have you not noticed that when you speak what you feel, just as when you do what you feel is right, that you are free? Also when you speak that which does not meet with the sanction of your innermost feelings, you feel you have limited or bound yourself.

This is the philosophy of non-resistance propounded by Gandhi and which is prevalent in Hindu teachings. Christ emphasized this teaching. When you speak or act in a manner that is out of harmony with yourself you create resistance and that resistance is the influence of hypnotic practices. It contracts the nature of man and keeps him from expressing what he truly is. Not only does this resistance occur in his own nature but, when brought to the notice of others, they further add to this resistance and by this practice the whole world is kept in darkness. "The Father who sees in secret rewards thee openly." No one resents the radiations of pure joy, even though they may be exceedingly sad, but try to talk them into joy and they resent it. Tell a poor man that he does not need to be poor and he is likely to resent it and will offer all sorts of excuses in defense of his poverty but bring him under the silent influence of abundance and his very soul expands. Try to separate two men who are fighting and they are likely to attack you but radiate a sense of peace from your own inner nature and they are more than likely to catch your sense of peace and cease fighting. The doctrine of non-resistance is not passive but is a dynamic radiation of the inner SELF.

Social reorganization and economic reform must emanate from the awakening consciousness of man. One cannot legislate or lay down rules that will govern man when under a spell of hypnosis. You cannot organize men's thoughts and motives until they conform to each other. It is in this realm that all differences arise. One man is selfish, another is unselfish. One is successful and another is a failure. One has unusual strength and ability, while another is weak and incapable. One thinks only of his material welfare and another thinks only of his spiritual welfare as entirely divorced from his outer nature. How can such diverging thoughts and feelings be organized into an harmonious mass? Only in man's innermost nature is he identical with his neighbor in thought and motive and only through bringing out what is within can there be peace and harmony in the earth.

It is that which moves in man's innermost nature that is identical with the great Universal Mind or God. "The law of God is written in your inward parts." Mastership is bringing to the surface what is buried within. This is brought about only through deep meditation and consulting with the SELF, which is the only master one can ever find that will lead him to the goal of life.

Overcoming is all a matter of learning to drop all seeming conditions of mind, body, and affairs and to begin life over again at its beginning. Start with the idea that you are that Self which you inwardly long to be and so devote yourself to being that Self that everything else is forgotten. Once you have found your Self and have become that Self, you are a master and a world helper. Many such working together in Silence will spread an influence over the world more powerful than any movements that originate in the machinery of organized industry, war, or social reform. The effectiveness of one's life is not so much in what he does but in how he does it and how he does it is determined by the degree of himself he has discovered.

Merely speaking words and relying upon the

power within them or the vibratory effect of the word never helps man to become a master. Words contain only that degree of power that is limited into them through the consciousness of the individual using them. The power is the depth of realization or the degree of consciousness back of them. It is not "words" that produce consciousness nor is it "words" that heal the body or change the affairs. It is a matter of awakened realization that produces words and impels outer action and the word or act is powerful only to the extent of this inner awakening.

The result of speaking or acting from outer motives not only produces an hypnotic condition of mind but gives rise to the notion that there are two opposing minds and, carried on, seems to divide the mind into many separate actions. Mind is a Unit and moves as a Unit and what seems to be dual-mindedness is only a dual set of ideas, one set evolved from outer impressions and one set originating in the natural state of mind as it originally moves. The mind is completely unified and harmonized by denial or rejection of every thought and impulse that does nto spring from one's innermost nature. This clears up the entire stream of consciousness and leaves the individual free to think and act as he should in perfect harmony with the Universal Mind. This is the very essence of mastery.

Speaking and living in this oneness without sense of division is the greatest gift of man for he was given "a sound mind", according to the Scriptures. In other words, he was started out into being in perfect oneness with his source; he was sound, whole, and Jesus said he must return to this state of sound-mindedness. "Tarry at Jerusalem until the Holy—whole—Spirit comes upon you" or until you return to that sense of oneness with the Universal Mind.

Spirit is Cause and when man returns to Cause, his Source, he becomes whole and sound. He is not only sound in mind but sound in body and his affairs become sound for his entire being is united into that great Unity which is the essential nature of all things. It is the soundness or oneness of all things in and with Source. Soundness or unity cannot mean anything less than the whole. It cannot refer to any individual or part of the whole. It must refer to the oneness of the whole. Everything is a center of unity or a center where the oneness of all things must be preserved and manifest. To localize or segregate any fact is to take it completely out of its nature and to lose its meaning altogether. When Christ spoke, "These and greater things shall ye do," or when Emil said, "You can do these things just as easily as I can do them," they were speaking from this consciousness of the only true unity, the soundness of the individual in his relationship to and with the whole.

This life of oneness is the life of the masters and anyone may live that life if he will drop his alliances with institutions and religions and races and nations and accept his alliance with the Universe. This is the "ark of the covenant" which enabled the Children of Israel to succeed but, when it was lost, they failed to gain their liberty from opposition.

All separation is purely a matter of individual hypothesis. One cannot really be separated from the whole for he is created within it, is a part of it, and is like unto it. Love is the great unifier in the consciousness of man and to keep oneself always in an attitude of love is to progress toward oneness. It is the only preserver of life and health and ability. One need not try to love everybody but he must eternally seek to keep his nature whole through the increase of love. When one's nature expands in love, he will sooner or later find himself in a loving attitude toward all men and, in this attitude, he not only lifts himself but all those around him into that same oneness. There are no divisions in an awakened sense of love.

One does not gain mastery or illumination by going to India and sitting at the feet of a master. One gains mastery by listening to the deepest facts of his own nature and by obeying what he there learns. There is no help that is needed that is not available instantly if one but turns in this direction and proceeds from this fact. All the power of the Universe is back of every high motive, every true impulse that stirs in man's inner nature. It is like the germ of life within the seed and all the forces of nature move to bring it forth into its full expression of all its potentialities. This is the manner of the masters and their instruction is always that you must be true to the Self, live the life of the Self, express what is inherently true until you are outwardly what you inwardly long to be.

When man returns to this motive of life, all that there is in the Universe begins to move in upon him, to manifest itself through him. Not only must man have the intelligence to direct him and the power to do that which is to be done, but also the substance that nourishes and supports him in the doing. There is no lack, except in the realm of hypnotic ideas that have clouded his mind from reality. Back in his native oneness, where he consciously receives what the Universe is pouring out upon him, there can be no lack in any phase of his being nor in his affairs.

The Quantum Theory is the approach of Science to this basic fact of life and there can be no true science, religion, social structure, or successful living outside the undefeatable and indissoluble oneness of all things.

This is the road to mastery, the life of the masters, and the only true life there is. It is to be found just where you are in the secret places of your own inner nature. The masters teach that liberation is to be found in this and in no other way. Christ, speaking in the man Jesus, said the same thing when he said, "No man cometh unto the Father but by me." The same Christ in you speaks the same message to you. Your only contact with a master is through the mastery in yourself.